P9-ASI-812

PATRICK J. O'CONNOR

ALL WORLDS POSSIBLE

THE DOMAIN OF THE MILLERS OF COOLYBROWN

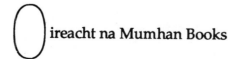ireacht na Mumhan Books

Published in Ireland by
Oireacht na Mumhan Books
Coolanoran
Newcastle West
Co. Limerick

Printed by Litho Press Co., Midleton, Co. Cork.

Contents

List of Illustrations

Figures

Plates

Preface

Holding within its embrace three generations of that fine family of the Millers of Coolybrown, *All Worlds Possible* may be described as a labour of love. As such, it requires no formal dedication.

However, many people have helped in making an idea take the concrete form of a book. For initially alerting me to the existence of the data on which the book is based, I wish to thank John McAuliffe, President of the Newcastle West Historical Society. For his generosity in making these data available to me and for his time, understanding and hospitality, I am indebted to Mike Ruttle of Altavilla, Askeaton, the inheritor of the Miller farm. When he first handed over a consignment of source material to me he exclaimed: 'You 're taking away my inheritance!' My best hope is that this book not only restores his inheritance but enriches and enlivens it. My thanks further extend to Mike's parents, Willie and Mary Ruttle, for their fund of Miller anecdotes and the vividness of their recollection.

Others helped too. In direct line of descent Emily Cliffe and John Ruttle may be cited, while among the ranks of old friends, neighbours and acquaintances of the Millers, the following names may be invoked: Jack Ahern, Johnnie Bennett, Jim Corbett, Maureen Donovan, P.J. Dundon, Michael Foley, the late Jim Heffernan, Denis Liston, the late Jim Liston, Jerry McMahon, Peg Mangan and Walter Ruttle.

As always, Dr. Chris O'Mahony, the Mid Western Regional Archivist, was unfailingly kind and courteous in fielding queries and supplying data, and I should also like to thank the staff of the Inter Library Loans Office at the University of Limerick, especially Mags O'Connor, and the staff of Limerick City Library.

Further afield the net of gratitude extends to John Alton in Wiltshire, England; Roy Doupe and Carolyn Heald in Ontario, Canada; and Professor Colin Lewis, Dr. Roddie Fox, Etienne Nel and Oakley West of the Department of Geography, Rhodes University, Grahamstown, South Africa. Back home, I was able to rely on the support of my wife Esther and of my children, Aisling and John.

Austin Bovenizer, Chairman of the Irish Palatine Association, took the front cover photograph with his customary flair and regaled me with his own reminiscences of the Millers. Bill O'Callaghan of Litho Press expedited the arduous business of book making with his usual blend of good humour.

Most of all, however, my gratitude goes beyond mortality to the departed Millers, their friends and relations who grace the following pages. They are the real makers of *All Worlds Possible* and in deference to them all, it is right that they should speak with their own voices. Editorial intrusion into their lives and letters is therefore minimised, apart from punctuation. The written language is allowed to keep all of its rolling rhythms and most of its mis-spellings, so that when spoken aloud it reflects accent, idiom and image - connotations of Irishness wafting through made worlds.

Introduction

1825, February 10.
MILLER Christopher, of Kilscannel, living at Cooley Brown
&
DELMEGE Barbara, of Killeheen, parish of Kilscannel, by licence and consent of parents[1]

I

In its way, *All Worlds Possible* is a remarkable memoir. It reaches back to tap the life and times of a farming household in nineteenth century Ireland and it reaches out to embrace the spread of family, friends and relations over far-flung corners of the earth. Emigrant spheres encompass a variety of settings in North America, South Africa, India and Australia. Thus it serves perfectly to exemplify the phenomenon of diaspora which came to characterise the Irish experience from *circa* 1850 onwards.

From start to finish, everything crystallises around the Miller family of Coolybrown. In this little known townland near Reens in Kilscannell parish in west Co. Limerick, the Millers farmed the same compact piece of ground with love and care for three generations. Occupancy is first clearly established in 1825. Then according to the local Church of Ireland register, Christopher Miller was already of Coolybrown when he married Barbara Delmege from the nearby townland of Killeheen. Their springtime marriage launched in effect a familial stake in the 53 statute acre farm that was to last till the late 1960s. At the time of their marriage Christopher was aged thirty and Barbara was nineteen.

They quickly settled down to the task of raising a family. Their first child was born on 21 March 1826.[2] He was christened Tobias five days later. Eight more children followed. Christopher, their second son, was born on 10 June and baptised on 29 June 1828. A third son, John, was born on 28 January 1831. He was later to die at the young age of twenty-two. Edward, their fourth son, fared worse. Born on 1 December 1833, he ended a short life on 20 February 1835. Another son also called Edward,[3] came next. He was born on 17 December

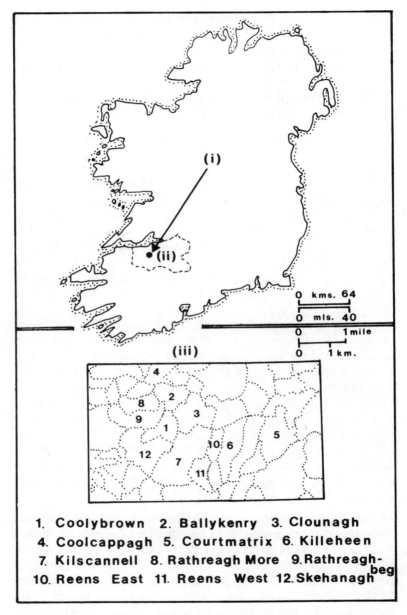

Fig. 1   Location within (i) Ireland (ii) Co. Limerick and (iii) the local suite of townlands

1836. Yet another son followed. Born on 7 February 1841, he took the name Robert at his christening a fortnight later. Two daughters then broke the male sequence, only to die young. Mary Anne was born on 9 March 1843, and died at three months. Emily was born on 13 January 1846, and died at the age of five. Lastly a seventh son and conspicuously the youngest, arrived on the scene on 17 March 1849. He was given the name Richard.

As invariably happened at this time, early mortality had taken its toll on a large family. Only five of the nine young Millers - Tobias, Christopher, Edward, Robert and Richard - survived to maturity. Among the five, however, there could scarcely have been more variability in the pathways they cut through life.

In 1846 we first encounter Tobias in attendance at road improvements near his home at Coolybrown. By 1849 he had risen to the rank of overseer of the Coolybrown works. Later he struck off for North America. Christopher too saw service at road maintenance, attaining the post of assistant overseer of the Kilscannell and Clounagh new lines in 1847, before joining the Royal Irish Constabulary. In 1852 he made overtures about emigrating to Canada, but eventually opted for a life in South Africa. At various dates in the 1860s and 70s we find Edward commissioning surveys of potato ground on the farm at Coolybrown and supervising its allocation among labourers. He stayed on at home in the capacity of relative assisting. Then in mid life he departed for distant Australia. From an early date Robert appears to have been identified as the prospective heir, a scenario which was signposted in his father's will in 1870. Alone of all the Millers, he stayed at home, married, and brought up a family. He lived to a ripe old age. Our earliest encounter with Richard comes while he was still at school, transcribing lines of proverbs in a flowing and elegant hand. He pursued yet another course by enlisting in the army in 1868. Soon afterwards he went off to serve imperial interests in India.

II

The Millers of Coolybrown came of impeccable Palatine stock. Their line of descent on Irish soil goes back to John Martin

Miller or Hans Martin Müller, as the German colonist of 1709 was originally known.[4] This may have been the Hans Martin Müller who married Margaretha Agnes Clöckner at Niederkirchen near Kaiserslautern in 1699; more research is needed to firm up a connective.[5] We are on surer ground, however, with the Rhineland exodus of 1709. That was when Hans Martin Müller along with his wife and four children made their own way to Rotterdam and sailed with the 4th party of Palatines to London. On arrival they were subject to a detailed enumeration which showed that the family head was aged 32, that he was accompanied by a wife, and by three sons and a daughter. The sons were aged 5, 6 and 8; the daughter was 2. Hans Martin belonged to the Reformed Church, and like four-fifths of his fellow colonists who settled eventually on the Southwell estate near Rathkeale in Co. Limerick, he fell into the occupational category of husbandman and vinedresser.[6]

Following on from his known movements in 1709, the progenitor of the Millers of Coolybrown was counted in Ireland in 1715 among a total of 213 Palatine family heads. In 1720 he was among the 103 heads of Palatine families to be enumerated on the estate of Sir Thomas Southwell and immediately after him in the listing came the name of Adam Miller. This was surely John Martin's eldest son who at 19 would have been old enough to head up a family in his own right.

Later on the Miller line and the Miller world is amenable to detailed reconstruction. Adam is registered as a freeholder of Courtmatrix in 1753 and again in 1776 and 1783. Here in this intimate setting alongside the River Deel about $1^1/_2$ miles to the south of Rathkeale the Millers had probably maintained a stake in land since the colonising phase of 1709-12. Courtmatrix is ranked as the oldest and most alluring of the Palatine parent colonies and Adam Miller spent the bulk of his long life there. He died in 1784, having been predeceased by his wife Mary twenty-one years earlier. They had as issue six or seven children, among whom Adam "Ye Younger" furnished the direct line to the Millers of Coolybrown.

This Adam was a freeholder at Courtmatrix in 1759 and one of the two of that name to be registered there in 1776 and 1783. In 1760 he married a neighbour's daughter, Juliana Shire. Thus he cemented ties within his own colony with one of the most populous of its clans. Adam and Juliana had six children born to them in the years 1762-82, with a baptismal record as follows: Anna, 17/4/1762; Christopher, 24/8/1766; Adam, 26/3/1769; Mary, 18/7/1773; Dorothy, 28/4/1776; and Jacob, 14/7/1782. Of these, Christopher the second born, upheld the ancestral line to the Millers of Coolybrown. Meanwhile the father and mother lived out their lives in Courtmatrix, where both died within months of each other in 1817. At the time of his death Adam was described as a tailor - a sure marker of marginalisation in an agrarian community.

Like his father before him, Christopher Miller opted for marriage with a neighbour's daughter. In 1788 he joined with Sarah Switzer at the Church of Ireland in Rathkeale and in doing so forged a matrimonial alliance with the most prolific of all the Courtmatrix clans. Seven children were born to them in the period 1790-1808, with the following baptismal record: Tobias, 13/3/1790; Mary Anne, 26/6/1791; Christopher, 11/1/1795; Tobias, 21/4/1799; Dorothy, 1/3/1802; Adam, 17/4/1803; and John, 17/1/1808. Christopher and Sarah lived in Courtmatrix when their last child was born in 1808, and Christopher was still recorded as paying tithes there in 1824.[7] However, they subsequently departed the scene. Christopher Sr. was of Waterfield[8] in the nearby parish of Clounagh on his death in 1837, while Sarah was with her son Christopher and his wife Barbara at Coolybrown when she died in 1853 at the age of 91.

In breaking away from the old core colony of Courtmatrix, Christopher Sr. may well have been following towards the end of his life a lead set by his son of the same name. That Christopher, as we have already seen, had migrated to Coolybrown in or before 1825 and there in splendid isolation from his own community he stood out in defiance of the usual Palatine wariness in landtaking. His two brothers, Adam and John, also opted for short-distance migration away from an overcrowded home colony. Adam was still of Rathkeale parish when he married Dora Bartman of Particles parish in 1839,[9] but they had removed to Clounagh to farm by the time their first child was born in 1840. Subsequent births confirmed them in residence at Laterville in Clounagh parish and at Ballykenry (fig. 2). Youngest brother, John, showed both learning and enterprise in his onward movements. In the 1840s we encounter him in charge of a classical school in Thomas Street, Rathkeale,[10] while in the 1850s, according to the Griffith Valuation, we find him farming 55 acres of land just north of the town at Kyletaun. Thus having broken clear of introspection on old ancestral ground, the Millers of the fifth generation had shown the capacity to strike out boldly. They were ready to take on the world.

III

In seeking to reconstruct the domain of the Millers, reliance is placed upon extant source materials. Such as are available survived in the Miller home at Coolybrown through as many as three generations of occupancy, before passing on in turn to a nephew and grandnephew of the last of the line. The range of the documentation is both varied and bitty. It is certainly incomplete - a point well exemplified in the patchy record of correspondence received. Parts of individual letters are missing, note taking is sporadic, and the keeping of accounts occurs in snatches. Tantalising questions arise as to what may not have survived the hearth fire or the bonfire. Still there is much to engage the eye and the mind, and from the fragments there is a story to be told.

Turning firstly to the home domain, a variety of sources await investigation. These relate to three main areas: family, farming and road improvements. In particular the overarching role of the family may be stressed, and identified in materials such as a family Bible, a will, numerous note books and account books, a school copybook, an army enlistment notice, and a broad range of incoming correspondence. The area of farming is also well served, with records which attest to livestock and cropping patterns, hired labour, land tenure and land surveys, income, expenditure and improvements. As for the third area of road-related work, it is restricted in scope to two attendance/account books and other fragments in the period 1846-62, when life at home was hard and chances few.

Turning to the domain away from home, emigrant letters provide the data. Such letters come from overseas spheres which open up sequentially and reveal the experience of family, relatives and friends. They also point to the existence of social networks and are useful for the purpose of cross-referencing. North America comes first in order with a total of seven letters.

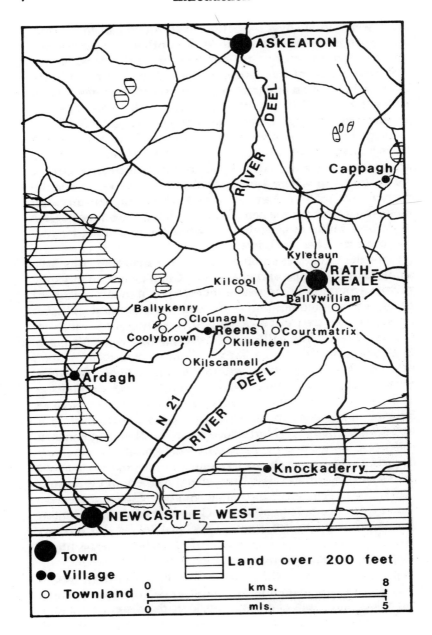

Fig. 2   Coolybrown in its regional setting

These were written over the period 1852-84 and gathered within their authorial embrace an uncle, a brother, a cousin and a friend of those in receipt at Coolybrown. South Africa comes next with a total of five letters or parts thereof, written in the 1850s and 60s by an emigrant son. This was Christopher Miller who after a spell in private employment became, through government service, a participant observer of a great land then in the making. From there the focus shifts to India where in the 1870s Richard Miller saw army service. Five of his letters home are extant. Last in order comes the antipodean world of Australia from where twenty-five letters, written over the period *circa* 1855-93, have survived wholly or partially. Of these, three are from the pen of James Winter, the brother-in-law of Barbara Miller of Coolybrown, while the remaining twenty-two come from her son Edward.

From the foregoing summary of source materials, this little study takes its shape and character. Chapter one surveys the narrow ground of home where there is much evidence of hard times, heavy outgoings and oppressed states of mind. Though possessing the credentials of snug farmers - 53 acres valued at £43.65 - life for the Millers of Coolybrown was a struggle. Emigration provided a palliative. Chapter two focuses upon new world horizons where, within the larger context of family, relatives and friends, the emigrant trail led to such destinations as St. Mary's in Blanshard township in Canada West; Kelley's Springs in Alabama in the American Deep South; Buffalo in upper New York state; North Bellerisa in the New England state of Massachusetts; and the great gathering ground of New York city. In chapter three the focus switches onto South Africa and places such as Simon's Bay, Knysna and Katberg in the Cape of Good Hope. Here amid a colonial situation Christopher Miller found fresh frontiers to subdue. Chapter four sees the setting moving onward to India where Richard Miller did military duty. He was with F Company of the 62nd Regiment. In chapter five the great raw world of Australia commands the stage, and the letter writers from the antipodes may best be characterised as traversing the outback. Chapter six recounts transitions in Ireland and in the world as the second generation of this family of Coolybrown gave way to the third. Then to tie up loose ends and to conclude, there is an epilogue.

Chapter One

The Narrow Ground : Ireland 1845-1893

John Miller is my name and Ireland is my station[1]

I

And a hard station it was too. Not long after he had written these words, John Miller was dead at the age of twenty-two. Like his brothers, Tobias and Christopher, John was involved in the arduous task of road making/improvement near his home at Coolybrown where - to judge from the timing - there may have been an element of famine relief in the works. He is specified as being in attendance for $24^1/_2$ days in November 1846 and for one day's horse work. After that, however, he failed to register an appearance, other than for his bold proclamation issued above.

With his elder brothers and his father, it was a different story. They were much more fully involved in the various works which seem to have dragged on sporadically over the period 1846-50. Tobias was in attendance all through November 1846 and in November 1849 he is described as overseer of the Coolybrown works[2] done with the authority of the local landlord, George M. Maunsell, of Ballywilliam, Rathkeale. In work carried out under his supervision the needs of drainage were paramount. It included sinking a main drain on his own farm at Coolybrown, sinking minor drains at a cost of $4^1/_2$d. (2p.) per perch and having horses draw stones to minor drains and to a sub main drain. Tobias remained committed to road improvements at least until the week ending 28 June 1850.

Christopher Miller Jr. first breaks on to the scene in March 1847 when he was appointed assistant to overseer, Denis Hogan, in the maintenance of the Kilscannell and Clounagh new lines (fig. 3). On 1 March, Christy Miller & Co. made 108 cubic yards of road-making material available at 7d. (3p.) per cubic yard; at another time they produced $113^1/_2$ cubic yards at 6d. ($2^1/_2$ p.) per cubic yard. These operations entailed the use of 29 and 22

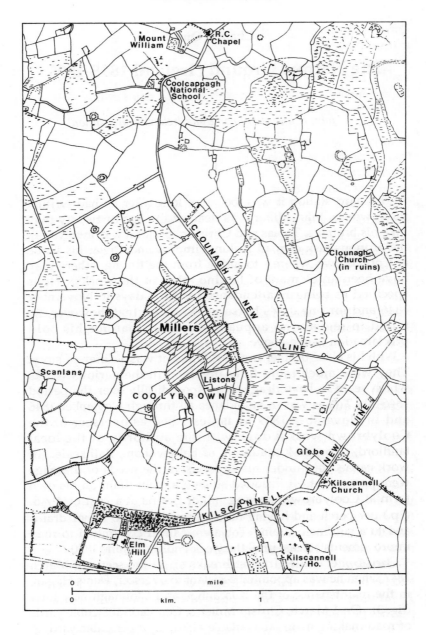

Fig. 3   The Miller farm in its local setting *circa* 1840

horses respectively. Later in 1849 and 1850 Christy Miller Sr. featured regularly in accounts for the hire of horses and men. Expenditure varied from time to time. At the lower end of the scale 9 men were employed at $4^1/_2$ d. (2p.) each per day; at the higher end 8 horses and 12 men required a day's outlay of £1.40. Christy Sr. retained his hiring role until at least 26 April 1850.

As well as playing a leading role in road improvements locally, the Millers also kept the tools committed to the works in their storehouse at Coolybrown. In this instance, available inventories serve as surrogates for the grind of the work undertaken and yield a kind of history that is handed up from the ground.[3] As of 3 April 1847, the following items were being stored for the Clounagh new line: 7 wheelbarrows, 4 handbars, 10 crowbars, 10 picks, 3 sledges, 34 stone hammers, 1 wedge, 3 jumpers, 4 mason's hammers and 5 blasting hammers. In addition 5 jumpers and 2 'poolers' were in the possession of Thomas Culhane, another assistant to the overseer. As of the same date, the following items were being kept for the Kilscannell new line: 2 handbars, 7 crowbars, 10 picks, 3 sledges, 36 stone hammers, 2 scoops and 2 wedges. Tools such as these held the promise of much sweaty labour for their prospective users.

And some measure of it emerges from the road books. In season the new lines generated a whole gamut of activity, including quarrying, blasting, boring, breaking, piling, filling, barring, drawing, fencing, levelling, cleaning, sinking, slooping and striping. The work of blasting and piling was computed in cubic yards, that of boring in feet and inches, and that of levelling and fencing in perches. Everything else was measured and paid for in days. The records are full of little insights like the 5 men who spent half of Monday, 17 September 1849, in the townland of Skehanagh cleaning the main drain in James Enright's land down to his turnip field;[4] or the 22 men in the quarry who still awaited payment for work they had done on Wednesday 31 October 1849; or the $6^1/_2$ perches of a ditch that had been levelled by Michael Liston[5] of Coolybrown by Monday 14 January 1850; or Christopher Miller's men who sunk 16 perches of minor drains in the week ending 26 April 1850.

The pay for all this was small. It was also seasonal and variable. For the men in attendance, daily rates fluctuated from a minimum of $4^1/_2$ d. (2p.) on the roads to a maximum of 1s.-8d.

(8p.) in the quarry. Daily rates for horse hire ranged from 2s. (10p) to 2s.-6d. (12$^1/_2$ p.). Stone and gravel was provided at between 4$^1/_2$ d. (2 p.) and 1s.-1d. (5$^1/_2$ p.) per cubic yard. The sinking of drains could vary between 1$^1/_2$ d. ($^1/_2$ p.) and 4$^1/_2$ d. (2p.) per perch. As well the works were highly seasonal, being most in evidence in the winter months of 1847 and 1849. Everything points therefore to the precariousness of life for those involved during and immediately after the Great Famine. Indeed for the men who quarried, blasted and bored etc., prospects at home can only have been at best meagre and at worst grim.

Corroborative evidence comes by way of members of the Palatine community who attended the works from the nearby townland of Killeheen (fig. 1). They included such contemporaries of the Miller brothers as Philip Stark (born 1825), Richard Piper (born 1826), Bowen Teskey (born 1826), Arthur Piper (born 1829), John Rynard (born 1830), Jacob Legear (born 1831) and Henry Stark (born 1832). All of these men came from among the ranks of the really pinched smallholders or the labourers. Philip Stark and Bowen Teskey were the sons of weavers - an occupation which by the time of the road works had almost completely lapsed. As for the rest of the Palatine contingent from Killeheen - George Bovenizer (probably the labourer of that name and not the farmer), John Bovenizer, Christy Legear, John Piper, Michael Rynard, P. Rynard and John Switzer - they also slotted in as smallholders or labourers in search of occasional employment. Joining them were much larger numbers of Gaels of the same lowly status from the townlands around Reen's Pike, and from the townland of Coolybrown John Hanrahan, Michael Liston and James Quaid swelled the ranks of those in uncertain employment for low and fluctuating rates of pay.

Years later road works were again on the local agenda when the tenants of Coolybrown were obliged by their landlord to undertake repairs or in default thereof to forfeit a total of £22.25. Such a sum would enable the landlord to pay for the necessary repairs leading from the high road down to Pat Hallinan's house. The date of the notice was 27 July 1862. By that time, however, the Miller brothers in attendance at the earlier works had all gone. John was dead, and Tobias and Christopher had emigrated to North America and South Africa respectively. Just how many more of their fellow workers opted for similar long distance trails away from a land of meagre chances must remain a matter for speculation! We can only be sure that the numbers were large.

II

Documentation pertaining to farming begins in 1845 against the unseen backdrop of the Great Famine. Once again, life at the margins may be spotlighted as female servants commence work on the Miller farm on specified days or accounts are furnished of the number of men in seasonal employment, the nature of their work, and the remittances paid to them. For example, Johanna Daly commenced service on 8 December 1845 and stretching out into the following year her duties entailed work in the tillage field, in the garden and in the bog, as she tended to the needs of wheat, potatoes and turf. At the same time other female servants such as Hanna Reddan, Mary Quaid, Margaret Daly, Catherine Molony and Nancy Burns were likewise engaged in the day-long chores of footing turf, binding wheat or picking potatoes. Men employed in the course of the 1845 season put in some 90 days work at rates varying from 6d. ($2^1/_2$ p.) to 10d. (4p.) per day. Out of the total, 26 man days were spent at wheat, 12 at turf, 9 at potatoes, 7 at skinning, 5 at oats, 4 at flax, 4 at digging fallow, 3 at 'drawing' and 2 at hay.

Dependence upon casual labour appears to have declined significantly thereafter. In 1846, for instance, only 15 man days are specified: 9 at reaping wheat, 4 at reaping oats and 2 at making hay. Later on, we learn that a solitary casual labourer, Daniel Eaton of Killeheen,[6] earned a total of 18s.-6 d. ($92^1/_2$ p.) during August 1858 for setting cabbage, drawing turf and hay, picking potatoes, fencing and reaping. As before, fixed term labour retained a place in the farm economy. However, here too there is evidence of a diminishing market as the record of commencements for servant boys and servant girls grew thinner over time. Rates of pay remained low, and varied with the individual bargains struck. In the 1870s and 80s, for example, wages for 12 months ranged from £3.50 for one Michael Murphy to £8.50 for one John Walsh, while at base, all William Delane could claim when he commenced service in July 1877 was a paltry 50p. a quarter.

Part of the reason for a contracting labour force lay in the swingover from tillage to pasture. This phenomenon is well known at national level in the second half of the nineteenth century[7] and is exemplified by trends on the Miller farm. In 1845 the pattern of production with its emphasis on cropping and mixed farming accorded well with prevailing land usage and with the Palatine traditions in landworking. The sheen of Sunday blue from the flax flower still lit the fields of Coolybrown alongside stripes of ripening wheat and oats. However, the Famine proved a decisive watershed as flax disappeared without trace and the limits of cultivation receded.

By the time Christopher Miller's son had taken over, things had changed radically. Tillage had been much reduced. The role of the 'big plough' was curtailed. This was in the 1870s when the cowman in Robert Miller had relegated the ploughman in him to a secondary role. Evidence comes by way of a series of livestock inventories which suggest that, even allowing for some landtaking in the townland of Kilcool in Doondonnell parish (fig 2), the lead of cow over plough was unassailable. At maximum in the January of 1881, 93 head of cattle were enumerated, which consisted of 41 cows 'strippers and all'; 13 in-calf heifers; 1 heifer not in calf; 5 bullocks coming three years; 5 bullocks coming two; 5 heifers coming two; 15 bullock calves; 1 bull calf; and 7 heifer calves. Added to these were 9 horses, 6 sheep and 4 breeding sows. In the newer leaner Ireland the dominance of livestock was emphatic and the demand for labour from inside the family as well as from without was much reduced.

There were, however, needs to be met at every turn, and by far the most ubiquitous note struck in the Miller data relates to the heavy burden of recurrent expenditure. Handsomely topping the bill were the landlord's rent demands which fell due for payment in March and September of each year. The earliest available data pertain to 1845 - the first of the famine years - when a half yearly rent of £17.66 was set for the 53 acre farm. This figure prevailed through the hard years until 1850 when it underwent an increase of over 80 per cent to £32.05. And so it held until the data lapse in 1852, by which time the combination of arrears and abatements in the Miller rent book suggests some measure of hardship. There can be no doubt in any case that the rent demands of Irish landlords were considered onerous. That much is clear from incoming letters to the Coolybrown household during the 1850s and 60s from spheres as diverse as Canada West, the American Deep South, and the Cape of Good Hope in Southern Africa.

By the time rental data next become available, the most far-reaching piece of land reform enacted for Ireland in the nineteenth century was finding expression at local level.[8] This was the Land Act of 1881 which sought to legalise the three Fs: fair rents, fixity of tenure and free sale. As far as the Miller farm was concerned, its most immediate manifestation came by way of rent reduction. According to a notice dated 21 July 1882, Robert Miller's last rent had amounted to £66.89. Under the new terms, a reduction of £19.89 was allowed. In future therefore his rent would amount to £47, to be paid in two annual moieties. However, notwithstanding the reduction and the apparently expansive nature of his livestock enterprise, Miller still felt the weight of the rent bearing down upon him. The evidence comes almost as a throwaway on a piece of paper specifying improvements (plate 1). *Circa* 1891 Bob Miller declared: 'I could never pay the rent of the farm only for the money I received from my brother from Australia for the past 14 years - by instalments, also by my wife's fortune.'

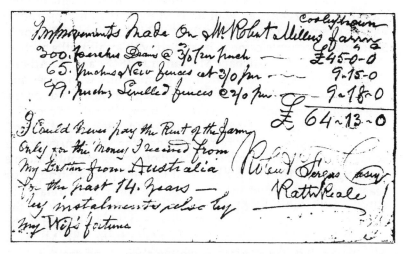

Plate 1   A throwaway piece of paper specifying improvements *circa* 1891

On a continuing everyday basis there was, of course, the provision of food and other necessaries, of which glimpses emerge in the Miller data. For example, the following is set out on an unspecified date *circa* 1850: 1 loaf of bread $2^1/_2$ d. (1p.), 3 lbs. of sugar 1s.-$1^1/_2$ d. ($5^1/_2$ p.), 1 quart of porter 7d. (3p.), 1 stone of meal 1s.-8d. ($8^1/_2$ p.) and 3 lbs. of meat 2s-$11^1/_2$ d. (15p.). The bill is totalled and marked paid. Paying their way, scrupulousness and honesty were the hallmarks of the Palatine people. So also was frugality, of which a telling illustration is furnished in 1876. Then in the months of July and August the only items of food to be procured were tea, bread and sugar. At other times the needs of cattle demanded attention, especially in the calving season. In the period February-April 1880, for example, $3^1/_2$ cwt. of Indian meal, 2 cwt. of pollard and $1/_2$ cwt. of bran were secured. Altogether four separate consignments of Indian meal are specified and some may conceivably have been included in the household food. A diet in which Indian meal featured could certainly mask thrift, as it did among substantial tenant farmers in the west Limerick hill country in the 1860s.[9] It could also be an indication of difficulty in making ends meet.

Other items of recurrent expenditure included smith work, payments to the surveyors of scoreground,[10] contributions to the parish collection of the Church of Ireland at Kilscannell, and the clothing of servants as well as feeding and founding them. Details of smith work are liberally sprinkled through the records as itemised accounts came to be settled with local smiths such as Pat Bourke (1845), Michael McNamara (1847) and T. Adams (1888). The needs of horses figured prominently with shoes and removes, while plough repairs and repairs to items like doors, gates and farm implements surfaced intermittently. Secondly, land surveyors such as William Nash (1864, 1868 and 1871) and Francis Walshe (1885) required fees for their surveys of scoreground. Thirdly, in the 1880s whole series of contributions ranging from 1d. ($1/_2$ p.) to 2s.-0 d. (10p.) on a Sunday or feastday are recorded in favour of the Church of Ireland in Kilscannell where the Millers went to worship. Lastly on the home front and again in the 1880s, itemised details related to the employment of servants such as Mary Lane and Michael Murphy spelt out *inter alia* their clothing needs and costs.

In contrast to expenditure, data relating to income are scant.

Earliest indications attest to the possible significance of tillage. Oats and wheat, for example, accounted for well over half of earnings of £68.15 that are specified in 1845. Pig sales on the other hand reached a modest £4.85. Later on, when grass management had come to dominate, cattle sales formed a significant component in the farm economy. This is suggested by the continuous oscillation in cattle numbers and by such snippets as the 8 two-year olds sold at the fair of Newcastle on 1 April 1881 or the 6 bullocks and 1 in-calf heifer sold at the fair of Rathkeale three days later. However, at a time when the cow was clearly queen, there is nothing at all of earnings from dairying. At least one other source provided income on a continuing basis. This was the allocation of scoreground among undertenants. In 1864 it realised £5.44; in 1866, £4.64; in 1868, £6.49; and in 1885, £3.25.

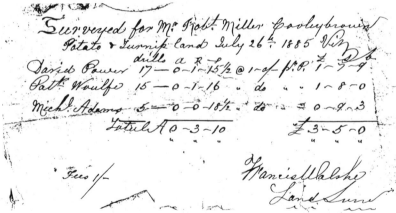

Plate 2   Survey of potato and turnip ground, 26 July 1885

The dearth of data makes it impossible to measure income against expenditure, except perhaps to venture that life may have been taxing for what passed as a snug farm family. Their atavistic impulses in any case would have stretched them. With the Millers as with their Palatine brethren, the idea of productive industriousness underpinned their attitude to life. And so even in a less than congenial milieu under landlordism the Millers assiduously farmed their own 'kind piece of ground.'[11] Their receptiveness to improvement is clear in the early days of the Kilscannell and Clounagh new lines when the

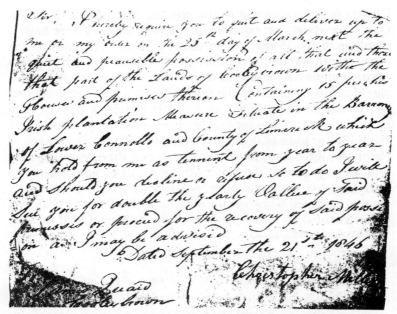

Plate 3   Notice to quit directed at James Quaid, 21 September 1846

needs of drainage on the home farm commanded the attention of Christopher Sr. and his son Tobias. Robert carried on in the same vein. In 1885, for example, he undertook the scouring and sinking of 190 perches of drains, while levelling 24 perches of ditches and removing 43 perches of banks. He also built a stable 18 feet X 14 feet, 9 feet high, with 2 gables and 2 doors. Later *circa* 1891, a further series of improvements are outlined: 300 perches of drains at 3s. (15p.) per perch, 65 perches of new fences at 3s. (15p.) per perch, and 99 perches of levelled fences at 2s.(10p.) per perch. The bill totalled £64.65 (plate 1). Normally this could be offset against the landlord's rent and so there was at least some compensation for effort on the part of the tenant farmer as well as the fruits that would accrue from his improved situation.

There was scarcely anything for the lowly undertenant. Holding at will or by the year under a farmer, they knew all about life on the margins. An early instance is furnished in a notice directed at James Quaid of Coolybrown in 1846. This humble labourer was to quit a minuscule piece of property by March of the following year or else face punitive sanctions[12] (plate 3). The renters of potato and turnip ground experienced the same pangs of insecurity. Their temporary little stakes in land were numbered in drills and measured and paid for in roods and perches. All they had was the promise of a crop and their chances for the season.

III

In homing in more specifically upon the life and times of the Miller family over the period 1845-93, one piece of evidence claims clear precedence. This is the last will and testament of Christopher Miller Sr. which was made in 1870 and which serves as a key marker of transition. Care and deliberation went into it and the witnesses John Miller of Kyletaun and Jacob Delmege of Killeheen, his brother and brother-in-law, were also the executors. Everything in the first instance - farm, furniture, livestock, implements - was bequeathed to his dear wife, Barbara Miller, subject only to the usual payment of debts, as well as funeral and testamentary expenses. All would then transfer to his son Robert upon entering a marriage that satisfied the two executors. In such a situation Robert's mother would be given an annuity of £5, together with a cow and the requisite feeding. She would keep her own room in the east end of the house. Upon marriage Robert Miller was to pay the other remaining son at home, Edward, the sum of £50 and support him for as long as he should remain unmarried. Should Robert die unmarried, the farm would go instead to Edward. Thus the will covered all contingencies to guarantee the smooth transfer of the farm, ensure (as far as possible) its perpetuation, and see to it that provision was made for other family members.

To uphold the integrity of the farm, there was to be one inheriting heir. The rest of the family had to be dispersed, or stay at home as a relative assisting, or perhaps despite being landless, marry into a farm. With such narrow options, emigration proved to be by far the most efficient filter of dispersal and in the Miller case, three of the five surviving sons had spread out upon the world, ever before their father had made his will. Tobias, the eldest, probably led off, followed by Christopher, the second born, followed by Richard, the youngest of them all.

Following on from his time in charge of road improvements

near home, Tobias proved to be the most shadowy of the Miller brothers. This is because there is no further direct documentation pertaining to him; none of his letters are extant. Nevertheless, at an early date his uncle, Adam Miller, made an overture about his coming to Alabama along with the youngest members of Adam's own family. Free passage upcountry was promised from the port of New Orleans. This was in August 1853, but as to whether or not Tobias took up the offer is unclear. What is certain, however, is that he did emigrate to North America. He was the subject of numerous enquiries over the years and when eventually news of his death was broken in 1865, it came from his uncle, Edward Delmege, who had settled at St. Mary's in Blanshard township in Canada West.

Christopher too was drawn away, having served as assistant overseer on the Kilscannell and Clounagh new lines in 1847. He went on later that same year to join the Royal Irish Constabulary[13] and in August 1852 we find him stationed in or near the post town of Bandon in west Co. Cork. Already he had made soundings about emigration as he sought the views of his uncle, Edward Delmege, on the merits of resigning from the Irish police and joining the constabulary forces in Canada. There was a decisive lack of enthusiasm for the idea. Constabulary forces in Canada were confined to the larger towns, had few vacancies, and a great many applications whenever posts became available. With farming, however, it was different, and an attractive scenario was framed for the prospective immigrant farmer.

In the event, Christopher was not tempted by Canadian prospects. He opted instead *circa* 1858 to go to South Africa, while entertaining the notion of proceeding to Australia where his aunt Thirza, a sister of Edward Delmege's, had settled along with her husband, James Winter.[14] Thus with relatives on two continents, Christopher eventually opted for neither. Instead he went his own way and had good reason to be grateful for his adventitious sense of timing. As he wrote home from South Africa:

> Dear Mamma, Now I may truly say that the Lord has directed my goings by not proceeding to Australia in that ship [in which] I emigrated. The Floune? sailed from the Cape of Good Hope on the second of July and on the 21st November she sprung a leak and was drowned.

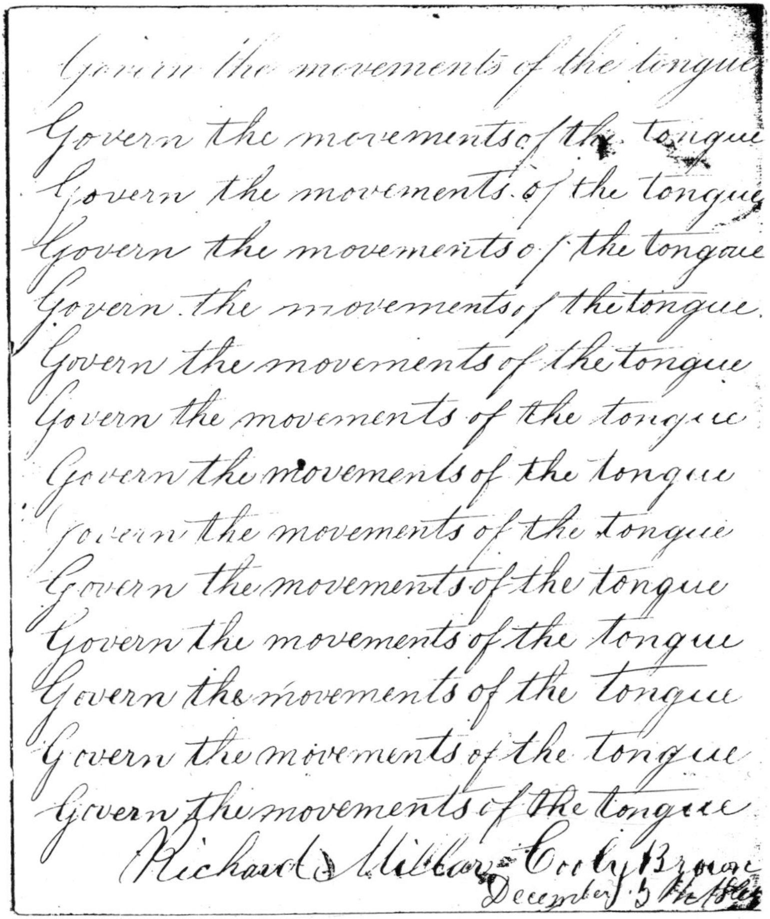

Plate 4   Richard Miller transcribing, 5 December 1864

Out of 150 souls aboard, including passengers and crew, only three regained the land. The rest met a watery grave.

With the departures of Tobias and Christopher, the three younger brothers remained on at home where much of the attention was focused upon Richard, the baby of the family. From South Africa, Christopher asked insistently that his dear young brother be kept at school. In the course of time he would take a trip home and bring Richard back with him. Meanwhile, learning would bring its own rewards and through the agency of an extant copybook we encounter Richard at school *circa* 1864, transcribing pages of headlines in a mode familiar to many of us (plate 4). His hand is neat and cultured and just a little ostentatious, as he writes out such aphorisms as:

Adversity often teaches wisdom
Govern the movements of the tongue
Labour assiduously at your calling
Humanity is an admirable virtue
Intemperance is a despicable vice

Still for all his learning and penmanship, there was nothing for him when he left school other than selling his own labour.

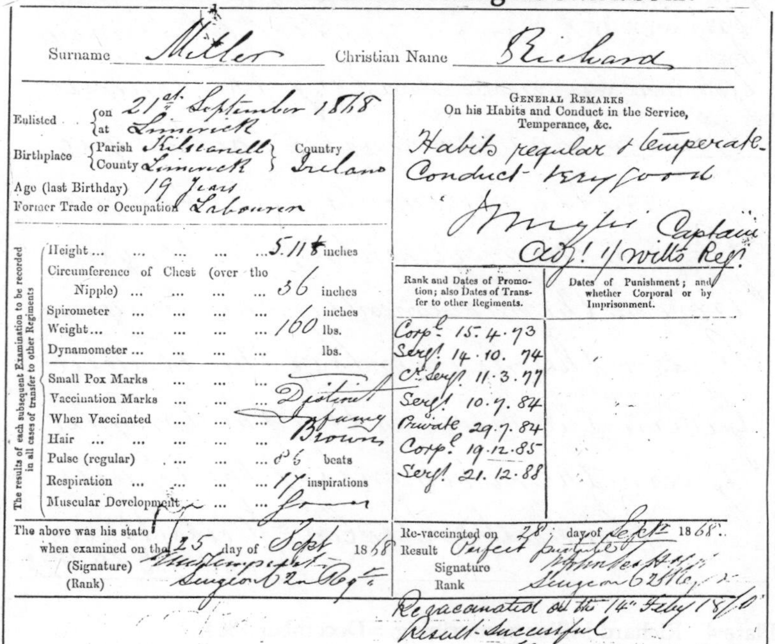

Surname Miller Christian Name Richard

Enlisted {on 21st September 1868 {at Limerick
Birthplace {Parish Kilscanell {County Limerick } Country Ireland
Age (last Birthday) 19 Years
Former Trade or Occupation Labourer

GENERAL REMARKS
On his Habits and Conduct in the Service, Temperance, &c.
Habits regular & temperate. Conduct very good
Captain
Adjt. 1/Wilts Regt.

The results of each subsequent Examination to be recorded in all cases of transfer to other Regiments

Height ... 5.11 inches
Circumference of Chest (over the Nipple) ... 36 inches
Spirometer ... inches
Weight ... 160 lbs.
Dynamometer ... lbs.
Small Pox Marks ...
Vaccination Marks ... Distinct
When Vaccinated ... Infancy
Hair ... Brown
Pulse (regular) ... 86 beats
Respiration ... 17 inspirations
Muscular Development ... Good

Rank and Dates of Promotion; also Dates of Transfer to other Regiments.
Corpl. 15.4.73
Sergt. 14.10.74
Cr. Sergt. 11.3.77
Sergt. 10.7.84
Private 29.7.84
Corpl. 19.12.85
Sergt. 21.12.88

Dates of Punishment; and whether Corporal or by Imprisonment.

The above was his state when examined on the 25 day of Sept 1868
(Signature)
(Rank) Surgeon 62nd Regt.

Re-vaccinated on 28 day of Sept. 1868.
Result Perfect
Signature
Rank Surgeon 62nd Regt.

Revaccinated on the 14th Feby 1870
Result Successful
Surgeon 62nd Regiment

N.B.—This endorsement to be filled up, and the Sheet transmitted to the Army Medical Department as soon as the Man ceases to belong to the Service.

Plate 5 Richard Miller's enlistment in the army, 21 September 1868, and his subsequent record

And it was the humble calling of labourer that Richard took with him when he went to Limerick on a September day in 1868 to seek enlistment in the army (plate 5). As with the police force, the army was often seen as a suitable outlet for a non-inheriting son. Richard enlisted in the 62nd Regiment Foot on

21 September and two days later he was to return to the Castle
Barracks in Limerick to be attested before a Justice. This would
complete the process of induction. Thus at the age of nineteen
the young man from Coolybrown had embarked upon an
outward-looking career. It was to take him off to India,[15] a
venture that was by no means greeted with approbation within
the extended family. As his cousin, Ann Miller, put it when
writing home from Buffalo in 1870:

> We were very sorry Richard [had] to join the army. I should
> think that he could get some better situation in life at home
> than to go out to India under the burning suns for low pay.
> But I hope he will soon raise in his ranks to be something
> high.

In truth, there was too little to engage him. The army offered a
way out.

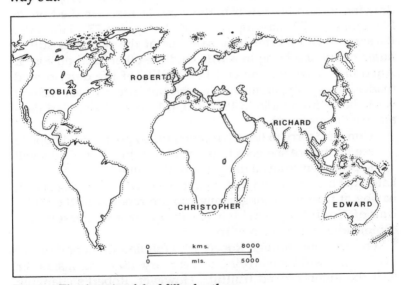

Fig. 4   The domain of the Miller brothers

One after another therefore the sons of Christopher and
Barbara Miller departed, away from a homeland of meagre
chances. The leave-taking clearly went hard on ageing parents.
So did the irreparable loss of a son, and when Tobias died in
1865 an emotional realm was forged which latched the
hinterland of exile onto the hearthland of home. From South
Africa, Christopher offered solace.

> It is with the fullness of heartfull sorrow that I have read the contents of my uncle Edward's letter. I cannot describe to you , dear mother, what or how I felt at seeing the account of my dear brother's death. But the will of the Almighty Be Done. I hope the poor fellow is happy and gone to a better world. All that I can say, dear father, mother and brothers, that though far separated in this world, if it shall be the will of God that we shall no more meet on earth , I hope in heaven, where parting is no more. May God comfort you all, my ever dear parents and brothers, for you have had your own share of trouble in this world.

He concluded with the hope that his parents were already much consoled.

However, advancing years brought few consolations and, when the old head of household made his will in 1870, he was drawing inexorably towards the close of life. He died on 26 November 1872, having attained the age of 77. His wife, Barbara, lived on after him, saw one of the two sons still at home marry and bring in a wife, and the other head off for far Australia. Towards the end her quality of life deteriorated markedly, as is apparent from a series of letters which Richard wrote home from India in 1877-9. On 1 June 1879 her last days are fixed in his mind.

> I am very sorry to hear that mother is so poorly but I hope to see her before she goes to the realms of Joy, if its God's will to protect us from all danger and difficulties.

Later that month the old matriarch passed away at the age of 73, having at least lived long enough to see renewal of the Miller line of Coolybrown which Christopher and herself had commenced over half a century earlier.

Renewal came through Robert who fulfilled the conditions of his father's will by marrying in February 1877 and inside the year the union proved fruitful. However, Robert's changing status had profound implications for Edward, the other remaining son at home. For him the whole weave of family life had changed. Moreover, the terms of their father's will made for an uneasy relationship between Edward and Robert, and by June 1877 word had reached Richard in India that the stay-at-home brothers could not agree. As a consequence Edward had left for Australia. Later on 9 July 1877 Robert duly paid over to Edward £50 sterling as had been stipulated in their father's will.

Receipt is acknowledged and any further claims are waived. The precise mechanisms by which this was done are not known because at that stage Edward had presumably reached Australia. He was certainly there by 9 August 1877 when he wrote home from Melbourne and prefaced his letter with the following:

Many places I have been and long since I have been a rover. I will go home and marry at home and be no more a rover.

For a man rooted in locality for all of the 40 years of his life up until then, the roving spirit of the Irish emigrant seems to have gripped his imagination immediately.[16]

In contrast, his brother, Robert, with whom differences were soon patched up, stayed resolutely committed to farm and neighbourhood for all of a long life. Even at an early stage he appears to have been identified as the presumptive heir because Christopher, writing from South Africa *circa* 1858, states:

I would send for Robert but I know that ye cannot do without him. If I had him here, I could at present give him £50 per year and more in a short time.

Later a clear signal of intent was given in the old father's will of 1870. Robert was to be favoured with inheritance of the home place, subject to entering upon a satisfactory marriage. He took his time about it and when eventually he did face the nuptial altar, his marriage to Anne Miller of Ballycahane in the parish of Kilcornan had all the appearance of a made match.[17] For one thing, it was a marriage between cousins. For another, the bride brought a dowry with her. Anne Miller and Robert Miller were married in Kilcornan parish church on 8 February 1877. Anne was 26 years of age while Robert was 36, having attained his last birthday on the eve of the wedding.

Afterwards it transpires that Robert's brother Edward may have been instrumental in making the match with Anne. He certainly held her in the highest esteem. As he wrote to Robert from Australia in September 1882:

Tell your dear wife I shall give her the first place amongst her sex and that I shall never forget her kindness for times gone by. Hoping ye will live long enough to enjoy a fruitful attachment as you both had for one another. One thing I feel happy for is that I acted the part of making two hearts one, which I could see was both your wishes.

He wrote as well to Anne in her own right and over the years he was most solicitous about her well being.

Through Edward's correspondence we can also trace a burgeoning family in the new Miller household at Coolybrown. In an early undated letter to Anne he responds approvingly to the first arrival.

> I enclose a feather for baby's hat and you can tell her she has an uncle in a far off land that will not forget her nor her mother.

Born on 24 November 1877, Barbara was to remain the undisguised favourite of her far-away uncle. She was followed by two sisters and a brother, and in June 1885 their uncle Edward again wrote expansively to their mother.

> I must say that you have not lost any time in regards as being fruitful and multiplying. The old house in Coolybrown will soon resound to the merry laugh and carol of the young Millers.

In April 1886 there are tokens from Australia for Barbara's two sisters, Emily and Mary Anne, and in June 1887 Edward promises to be a good uncle to Christopher, the first of his nephews. These four were to be joined by five others to make up the full family complement by 1894: Barbara, Emily, Mary Anne, Christopher, Edward, Rose Isabella, Clara, Robert and John Albert. With such a large family to cope with as well as numerous needs and responsibilities to be met, it is clear that Bob and Anne Miller were kept continuously on their mettle.

From the inside therefore it is easy to understand the perception of Ireland as narrow ground and symptomatic of it all comes Bob Miller's declaration of *circa* 1891 concerning his long-standing inability to pay the rent from his own resources. Substantiation from the outside is lent in his brother Edward's letter of July 1889.

> I am glad you have the rent paid ... About the 20th of next month I will send you £10 ... You will get the £10. It is not much but it may keep you going. You will get it in October and do not answer this letter till you get it.

Reliance on emigrant remittances is spotlighted here and there is enough of Ned Miller's Australian correspondence intact over the period 1877-93 to suggest that he was a generous benefactor to his encumbered family at home.

To these telling pieces we may add numerous emigrant perspectives which over the years mercilessly exposed a lean

and hungry land, full of pride and bigotry. Here it will suffice
to highlight the views of the Miller brothers: Christopher,
Richard and Edward. For Christopher, the thought of ever
again taking up permanent residence in Ireland would elicit
nothing less than a suicidal response. As he reported from
Katberg, Cape of Good Hope in July 1865:

> I am fully intent on going home to see you if spared by April
> next '66, to remain a short time. But to think to live in
> Ireland, I should as soon think of drowning myself as to
> remain in a land where people are so oppressed by landlord
> and other taxation and looked on by their superiors as the
> slaves by the landlord, which if the best of them were here
> are no better than any other person.

For his part, Richard is sore and tetchy about an unsustaining
homeland when asked as to how India agrees with him. From
Chakrata, he writes in April 1877:

> If any one wants to know about it, let them come and
> experience it, the cause as what I had to do myself, famished
> from the land of my birth.

Edward is much more forthcoming about Australia in his
lengthy and detailed letters, while he too castigates his
homeland. As he writes home to mother:

> Parties out here make no distinctions like old Bigoted
> Ireland. I wish to God that I came out 10 years ago, but
> better late than [n]ever.

Still for all that, Edward was alone among the emigrant brothers
in writing insistently from the start about returning some day to
Ireland for good.

That time came in 1893. Having never married and having
saved and invested wisely, he came home to Coolybrown
bearing gifts for his nearest and dearest kin - the continuing
occupiers of the narrow ground.

Chapter Two

New World Horizons : North America
1852-84

I wish you to send them as speedily as you can engage passage for
them on the first safe vessel bound to Mobile or New Orleans[1]

I

In order of chronology the oldest emigrant sphere to be revealed
is North America and the first letter encountered is one to
Christopher Miller from his uncle, Edward Delmege. Edward
was writing from St. Mary's in Blanshard township, Perth
county, Canada West, in 1852 and straightaway we are plunged
into a transposed Irish Palatine world because of the fact that
colonists from counties Limerick and Tipperary pioneered the
opening up of this township to settlement in the 1840s and 50s.[2]
Having been surveyed in 1839, Blanshard's first settlers were
tardy enough in arriving in 1841. Thereafter, however, it was
settled with great alacrity and many of the early Palatine
colonists were drawn from elsewhere in Ontario to settle down
together along the Mitchell Road, just north-west of St. Mary's
town site (fig. 5).

The migrants paid $2.50 to $3.00 per acre for their land; most
were required to take out a lease first, which generally lasted for
ten years and carried the obligation to perform settlement
duties.[3] For their part, the Palatines took to the task with gusto.[4]
In 1843 members of the much branched-out Sparling clan found
themselves in the van of a colonising drive that was to be
followed in the same year by the Raynards and the Switzers.
The Benners, Legears and Shiers came next in 1844. Then came
Delmeges in 1846, Doupes in 1847, St. Johns in 1848 and Millers
circa 1850. All the time existing clans were being strengthened
by the pull of chain migration, while the Ruttles, Brethours and
Teskeys were also to claim a representative presence. For some,
Blanshard represented a secondary phase of colonisation within
the province of Canada West as the sons of pioneering farmers

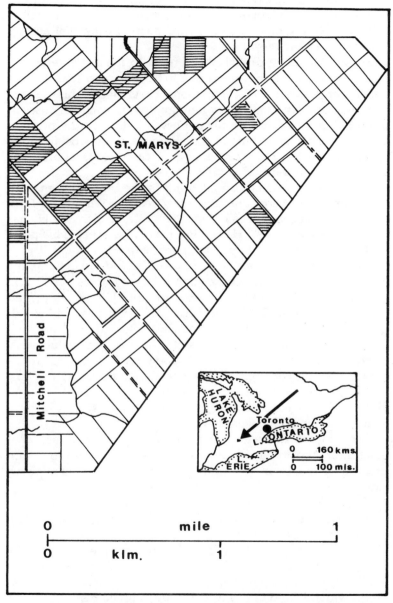

Fig. 5 Palatine settlement in and around St. Mary's, Blanshard township, Canada West, 1861 (adapted from Heald, 1994, forthcoming)

moved out to settle upon new land. For others, it represented a
direct move from Ireland as word spread among long-tailed
clans and the tug of kinship attracted them to congenial nesting
places in the New World.

Edward Delmege probably belonged to the latter category.
He appears as a relative newcomer to St. Mary's in 1852, having
taken over possession of a farm there. He is eager in his quest to
win over new land and is strongly guided by rural impulses in
formulating a response to his nephew's letter. In the process,
Delmege distils something of the ambience of a township in the
making,[5] while presenting a cogent case to his nephew as
prospective emigrant. He writes:

> Farming in this country I think is the best for a man to
> commence at here. For after a few years he will get his farm
> cleared and can live as independent as a gentleman. He has
> no rents tax to pay. He can kill his ox, his sheepe, his pork.
> He need not sell it to pay landlord rent. He can use it with
> his family, what cannot be done in Ireland. In general, the
> farmers are well off. I have about twenty acres cleared on
> my farm this winter. I intend to get 20 acres chop[p]ed
> down and cleared off in the spring. If I were to sell it I could
> double my money, but I do not want to sell, for I am well
> pleased with the situation. Land is increasing in value every
> year. Further improvement is going on fast and rail roads
> are making through all parts of the country, with every
> village marked places.

Here is a new land rich in promise as against an old land
weighed down with encumbrances.

Then Edward Delmege homes in on the push/pull factors of
emigration and in New World situations he goes on to assign
precedence to labour over capital. As he writes to his nephew,
Christopher:

> Had your father come out here some time past, with such
> good help he would be much better off, as help is better than
> money in this country.

No doubt words like these struck a responsive chord in the
minds of many family heads, who sold out their interest in Irish
land and took their families and whatever capital they had to
places with the kind of promise that are outlined here.

Everything that Edward Delmege writes is sober, sensible,
even laconic. The thoughts are those of a mature man. He is

hesitant about offering advice and states that 'a great [many] after they come here first gets home sick and are discon[ten]ted.' As for himself, he will admit to liking the country well and believes that he can do better in Canada than at home. Significantly he adds as a pointer to Palatine solidarity in exile that 'all the friends that came out are of the same opinion.' A man could earn from 15 to 20 dollars per month along with his board. There was work in plenty to be had. Specifically in relation to prospects in the police, his response is as follows:

> You want to know whether there are constabulary force[s] in this country. There is some and these are confined to large towns. It is not easy to join them as there is seldom vacancies and where there is, there is a great many applications. Their pay is from £75 to £100 per year.

He then proceeds, as we have seen, to express his own clear preference for farming as offering the optimal chance to the intending emigrant.

Towards the close he dwells on friends and family. He reports that Dan Ruttle from Askeaton was doing well, having been endowed with 'a good parcell of sons' who doubtless contributed handsomely in clearing off a fine farm. Again he refers to the well being of 'all the friends' who as transposed members of the Irish Palatine community accounted for about 5 per cent of the total population of Blanshard.[6] Richard [Delmege?] is reported as hiring with an old gentleman on Lake Erie shore and having little to do for good wages. By dint of chain migration he too was set to come to Blanshard. Then Edward turns to home and he seeks in answer to his letter word of his father and family. News of a recent marriage has reached him and accordingly he wonders if Christopher Miller has any notion of that kind himself. Relating marital status to exile, Edward recommends that a married man intent on coming to Canada had better bring his wife along with him. If on the other hand the prospective emigrant was single and without capital, he would be better off to stay single. On that cautionary note, the letter ends.

For his own part, Edward Delmege appears to have remained single because we subsequently learn from the next available census returns that he married in 1853. In 1861 he and his wife Eliza were enumerated at No. 1 ward in Blanshard township along with their children: Mary aged 7, Rebecca A. aged 5, and

Ellen aged 2. [7] Edward himself was then aged 39 while his wife Eliza was 30. Only once more do we hear anything of him. This was in 1865, when a letter of his reached Christopher Miller in South Africa after being mediated through Coolybrown, with news of Tobias Miller's death.

II

Moving from the loyalist world of Canada to an entirely different ethos in the Deep South of the United States, the next available letters come from the hand of Adam Miller. Already we have encountered this Adam on home ground as having broken away from the old core colony of Courtmatrix. In 1839 he upheld the bond of Palatine interconnection by marrying Dora Bartman of Glenosheen and we subsequently find them farming at Ballykenry in the parish of Clounagh where at least three of their children were born: Charles, 15/5/1840; Anne, 24/3/1847; and Tobias 7/3/1850. Two other children appear to have gone unrecorded: a boy named Christopher and a girl called Catherine. Tobias was probably the youngest of those born in Ireland.

From the first of his letters home in August 1853, it is clear that Adam Miller was a relative newcomer to the American Deep South. He had evidently gone off as pathfinder accompanied by his sons, while leaving his wife and daughters behind. Showing once again a predilection for rural settings, he settled in a place called Kelley's Springs in Alabama, which was located within range of the Gulf of Mexico ports of New Orleans and Mobile. From there he wrote to his brother Christopher, head of the Coolybrown family. The import of his letter is apparent straightaway.

> Inclosed I send you eleven dollars, supposing that amount together with what I have already sent will be sufficient to defray the expenses of my daughters to this country. Such matters [as] clothing as they may need for the voyage you will please procure for them as cheap as possible. I wish you to send them as speedily as you can engage passage for them on the first safe vessel bound to Mobile or New Orleans. If they go directly to Mobile send them to the care of Mister M. Lelland & Co. If to New Orleans, to the care of John T.

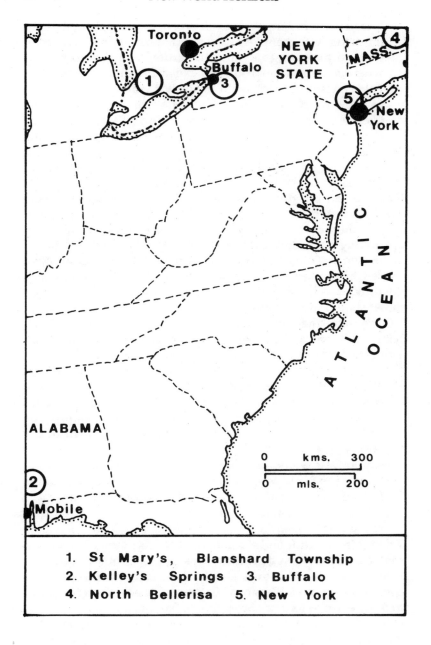

Fig. 6   The North American emigrant sphere 1852-84

Nardio, 70 Grasiere St., N.O. It will be well for them to bring this letter with them. As soon as you take shipping for them, write to me giving the time of starting, name of vessel and whether bound to Mobile or New Orleans. If your son Tobias wishes to come with the girls it will cost him nothing to come from New Orleans up as I will arrange with my friends at that place. I wish you particularly to charge Catherine to act sensibly and take especial care of Anna whilst on the ship. I shall feel under many obligations to you if you will go with them to Liverpool and see them safe on the boat.

Once he had put down roots therefore Adam's thoughts were fixed on restoring the integrity of his family and he sought to hasten the day of reunification by laying down plans with apparently meticulous care. He makes pleasing reference to two of his sons. Tobias, he reports, 'is now a stout healthy boy,' while Christopher 'is a stout boy and good worker and earning good money,' just as Christopher Sr's. own sons would, if their father should care to send them over.

Once more the allurements of life abroad are presented to a home audience, and like Edward Delmege in Canada, the letter writer from the Deep South pens a vivid picture of well being in a new and congenial environment.

We are all well and doing well, making abundant crops of corn, wheat, rye, oats, barley, potatoes etc. In short, we are a highly favoured people and I have great reason to be thankful that I am likely to succeed in getting all of my family to a country where I can make for them a decent support. It would be a happy thing for you and a pleasant thing to me if it were possible for you all to leave starving Ireland and come to a land of peace and plenty — We have a healthy, pleasant country, mild climate, steady and religious citizens.

Adam Miller had found a niche in what has been referred to as the Celtic South[8] and he was anxious that his brother's family as well as the rest of his own, should depart a 'starving' land and come to share in its blessings. In reply, Christopher's letter was to be directed to Kelley's Springs, c/o Samuel Jamison.

However, for all of Adam's expansiveness, organisation and entreaty, nothing was done. Consequently on 8 February 1854 he wrote again to his brother, Christopher, at Coolybrown, seeking clarification.

> You informed me the remittance of forty dollars I made was not sufficient to pay the fare of my children to this country without delay. I sent eleven dollars more which you should have received by 1st October last and of which I have had no account since it left New York. If you have received it I think [it] strange my children do not come or that I cannot so much as hear from them. On the reception of this you will please inform me immediately what has become of them and what has caused this long delay. You must know I suffer much uneasiness on their account and greatly desire to see them. If they are still in Ireland I hope you will consider your obligation as my brother and their uncle and use the necessary exertion to send them to me. If they have left there please let me know when, on what vessel, under whose care etc. If they have not left, start them immediately. Send them to the care of John Nardio & Co., New Orleans, who is instructed to send them to me. Inform me on what vessel they come, when they start etc.

The only other note added was a perfunctory 'we are all well.'

In shedding some light upon this entire episode, it is fortunate that the rough draft of a reply should be appended to the back of the above letter. Christopher Miller had received the letter on 10 March and his draft reply was dated 12 March 1854. Christopher lays the blame squarely with Adam's wife for his tardiness in sending out the children.

> You think it strange I have not sent your children to you and you would think it hard if I did not do you justice. —— Did your wife not tell you [about] her agreement with me when I kept her child. You left me none of your children. It was your wife [who] promised in the presence of witnesses to pay for the support of her child, but the ungrateful woman never has so much as acknowledged my kindness to her and [her] family after she came out of the workhouse.

Here is a clue that Adam had gone off, leaving his wife and daughters behind. They must have subsequently fallen upon the very worst of times since reference is made to a stay in the workhouse. Well might Adam Miller invoke in his earlier letter the phrase 'starving Ireland!' His brother Christopher had offered the hand of succour, but an agreement with his wife relating to child support had still to be honoured. Indeed the hand of succour had been bitten, as Christopher saw it.

> Since your wife has met you, you never said one word about my trouble. It appears she has proved as false there as she has here in villifying the characters of my family.

A sense of grievance therefore co-mingled with a deep sense of personal rancour.

Christopher also charged his brother Adam with promising, but not delivering, £40 for one year's support of their mother. She had presumably lived with Adam before his departure to America and had gone on to spend her last days with Christopher at Coolybrown. She died in 1853. This, however, merits mention only in passing. The real bone of contention is with Adam's wife.

> The fact is when your wife sends me what she has promised me I will send her children to her and not till then. The sooner the better, and anything you see wrong in me, your wife is the cause.

It is not known how resolution came. We only know that the matter was resolved, as the next sequence of letters shows.

III

Years later we find Ann or Anna Miller in Buffalo at the Lake Erie edge of New York state, from where this daughter of Adam of Kelley's Springs corresponded with her kinspeople in Coolybrown. Whatever about her older sister Catherine, it seems certain that Ann had spent her youth at Coolybrown. This is conveyed by the intimacy of her relationship with the people there and also by her abiding state of homesickness for Ireland. In this latter respect she was unique among all of the correspondents that flit across these pages, as we read what are in essence the texts of rural immigrants.[9]

Ann had married and settled in Buffalo, and her letter of 10 July 1870 sets the familial scene for those in receipt in Coolybrown.

> Dear Cousins, I would have written to you before now but I was waiting for to get a letter from my father. But he gives us no encouragement, only that we would have to work for our living there, the same as we have to do in Buffalo. I believe my father has no money, but having the land. He

> has 150 acres of land 2000 miles away from me down South
> and he wants us to go down to him. But it would cost 20
> pounds to go to him and I would sooner go home to Ireland
> with the money than to go South so far. Besides there is too
> many of themselves there. My brother Charley got married
> this summer and brought in his wife to the house. So
> Charley and his wife are in the house with the rest of them
> now. So I think there is enough of themselves there for to
> take up all the land.

It appears that Ann, then aged 23, was a relative newcomer to
the United States and that she had not been united with her
father and the rest of the family on their adopted homeground
in Alabama. Neither was there much prospect of an upcoming
reunion.

Rather she was drawn longingly towards Ireland, and despite
its obvious handicaps, towards occupancy of the land of Ireland.

> We may talk of land, but I would sooner 30 acres of land in
> Ireland than one hundred acres in America. The land out
> here is [of] a sandy nature, bare, barren looking land, half
> woods and swampy land and now at this time of the year
> the grass is burned up with the heat of the burning sun. But
> their land,[10] I hear, is a great property. You may call it real
> estate. There is no landlord to claim the rent and no taxes to
> eat your labour up. When you get land here you get it for
> ever and all your generations after you and I am sorry it aint
> so in Ireland. Yet there is no Irishman here but loves that
> land he left behind him.

She is rapt in thoughts of a green and pleasant land, to which
she yearns to return.

> Dear Cousins, Ann wants to go home to Ireland. Dearly she
> will not content herself here. She is so lonesome since she
> left her aunt [11] and hopes she will see her before she dies
> with God's help. So now, Dear Cousins, if we went home to
> Rathkeale next summer with 100 pounds and took a shop
> there, do ye think we could do well there to keep [a] flour
> store and publick buisness and grocery buisness in hands?
> Let me know in ye're next letter. So we wants ye're advice
> and if ye will not advise us to go home, we will stay here
> and settle down for life.

This all seems the written extension of a daydream rather than a
plan penned with conviction and expectation. She will be too

easily said by those at home. Perhaps it was just a way of dealing with the pain of exile in urban America - a turn of mind to obfuscate the grim reality of everyday living.[12]

Ann then proceeds to empathise with the Coolybrown family whose youngest son had recently gone into exile, and while she bemoans the fact that Richard had to join the army, she tempers this with the hope that he would soon rise in the ranks. In conclusion, she addresses her cousin Edward directly.

> Dear Edward, I am not forgetting the handkerchef. You make sure of it in your next letter, and a good one too. So do not be falling asleep in your next letter, but write us a good long one. We will send you some of the American newspapers in our next writing to you. So my husband and myself is sending our best love to ye all. No more at present from your affectionate cousin, Ann   Miller.

By way of a postscript, she asks that the reply be directed to John O'Connell, No. 110 North Division Street, Buffalo, State of New York.

Almost two years elapsed before Ann Miller's next surviving letter to Coolybrown. This was in June 1872 and she opens as she did previously with an account of her family in Alabama. It makes sad reading.

> Dear Uncle and Aunt, I have to inform you that my father is no more. He died on the 21st of last July 1871 and Charley's wife in June 1871 and Charley's baby died the same time. So they got enough of death in their family and we cant make out here in Buffalo what way the land is to be settled between the children. We are thinking that Charley will put them all out of it because John in 6 or 7 years was not at home and there is nobody to take hold of it but Charley. As for the rest of the children, they are young and we think the old man died without making any will. We cant say for a while. We expects a letter soon from my sister and then we will know all about it. There is one thing sure that my father had no money laid by. The War Down South ruined him and everybody else that lived there.

Death and circumstance conspired to completely upset the life of a farm family and in the process yield a fragment of the dispirited geography of the post-bellum South.

Following on from this sombre passage, Ann again addresses her cousin Edward directly and she proceeds to draw an adverse comparison between the land of exile and the land of home.

> Dear Edward, home is far superior to here. It is like a man going in to the city of Limerick to look for work and if he do not get work he must starve. Now here in Buffalo last winter we had 6 months of frost and snow. Now I would like to know where a man could get work for them 6 months and then if he do not get work he cant get wages enough to keep his family and himself right. I have seen some families here where I live and last winter I have seen them sending out their poor hungry children to the hotels to beg for victuals. Now at this time of the year everything goes lovely. You would think by the people that they would not ever see the frost or snow again, but as sure as the sun shines to-day the hard freezing that would freeze off your toe nails and your ears and fingers will be here next winter again. Dear Edward, the green Irish man that comes from Ireland would often cry to be back again in the old sod.

Even in summertime the very contemplation of the long North American winter filled the heart with trepidation and in the chronically homesick, such as Ann Miller, thoughts of the homeland induced an anguished state of mind. Come the winter, the condition was rendered all the more acute.[13]

Ann next engages in a spot of ethnic stereotyping. This too is revealing and interesting since, in the context of a city of mass immigration, it gives us an insight into popular perceptions of otherness.

> Dear Edward, you would like to see the Dutchmen out here and the Germans. There is 6 Dutchmen to one Irishman here in Buffalo and it is so all over. They are just like the Kerrymen at home and it would make you laugh to hear them speak English. You would not like to work amongst them. They're dirty class of people.

Judging from this, the development of the Kerryman joke would appear to have a layered and colourful history, while the us and them mentality of the immigrants' field is powerfully conveyed in ethnic hues and tints.

Transcending everything, however, Ann longs for a start at home.

> Dear Edward, will you do one thing for me? [That] is to tell me if we went home to see if we could make a living out of

100 pounds and to see could you get us a bit of land in your neighbourhood, and let me know if we bought some cows could we get grazing land for them or to keep dairy cows. Any way we could live there!

Keeping the focus on home, she wants to know 'all about the neighbours.' She enquires if Richard is writing and if he is still out in India, and she ends by asking that a letter in reply should be directed to John O'Connell, No 76 Effenor Street, Buffalo, State of New York.

IV

Yet for all her thoughts of home, there is no evidence to suggest that Ann Miller ever returned. Rather the trail continued to lead in the opposite direction and in 1884 we find Mary Anne Delmege,[14] another cousin of the Millers of Coolybrown, writing home from a small town in Massachusetts. News of Mary Anne's departure to America first filters through in a letter from Australia in 1883, when she was aged 26. By then, the family regime at Coolybrown had changed. Robert and Anne Miller were in charge and it is to the latter that Mary Anne's letter of 27 October 1884 is addressed.

Plate 6   The headed notepaper used by Mary Anne Delmege, 27 October 1884

My dear Anne, I am sure you will be [pleased] at the receipt of a letter from me after such a long time. However, better

late than never. I had my pictures taken and I am sending
you one. I hope you will get it alright and I shall be
expecting a long letter from you with all the news. I hope
you Anne, Bob and children are quite well. I am feeling first
rate just now, in fact better than I ever did in the old country.

Unlike Ann Miller in Buffalo therefore, Mary Anne took well to
her new life chances at North Bellerisa near Lowell in the state
of Massachusetts.

Like many a woman corresponding with another woman, she
is concerned about her personal appearance. Weight is viewed
as a sensitive index.

I am not quite so stout as I used to be. I always was too
stout. When I came to this country first I weighed about 180
lbs. and I got myself weighed yesterday and found I weigh
166 lbs. Dont you think that is quite a reduction? And I
hope I will reduce 20 lbs. more.

Clearly Mary Anne was feeling good about herself and was
finding her new life congenial.

She went further, detailing her work in, what was for many,
the familiar textile setting of New England. [15]

My dear cousins, I know you will be glad to know that I am
getting along splendid and never felt better than I do since I
came out to this country. I suppose you are aware that I am
not working at my trade as I like weaving much better than I
do serving in millinery and it is a better paying job also.

To finish, Mary Anne again reverts to topics touched upon
previously.

Now dear Anne, I will be expecting a long letter from your
dear self with all particulars. So dont fail to let me know if
you see a change in my picture. It is a good one of me. Now
I close with love to all and as many kisses as the post can
carry.

The warmth of fellow feeling between Mary Anne and her
cousins in Coolybrown is palpable and, thanks to the fortuitous
survival of a letter, we can still sense it deeply to-day.

V

The last of the extant letters from North America comes from
James Hackett of Springhurst, Ward 23, New York City, and it is

directed to Robert Miller at Coolybrown. Bearing the date 1 October 1884, it recalls in the first instance what appear to be both men's pre-nuptial days together in the employment of a local lady.

> Dear Robert, it is time for me to think of writing to ye after our long acquaintance together. Just a few lines about old times when we were with Sarah Gibbings.[16] I heard that Mr. Harney did not stay long with her. I always told you that she would not keep any one while she had Miss Jane. I suppose they are both together yet and will until they die. For they were two nice creatures and it would be a pity ever to separate them. I hope, dear Robert, that you and your family is in good health and also all the neighbours. Kate wishes to be remembered to your wife and also myself. We both join in sending ye our best love and blessings and is glad to have to tell ye that we are getting along splendid in this country.

As ever, the writer is solicitous about friends and neighbours at home and he is eager to point up his own successes abroad.

> Dear Robert, I wish to let you know the work that I am at for the last year. I am in the repairs of a railway at 9 dollars a week, wet and dry. It is hard to get a[n] easy job in this country and the heat is beyond all this year.

However, health is the controlling influence and Jim Hackett thanks God that he and his family never had a day's sickness since they came to New York.

Fond remembrances again surface when the writer inquires and surmises about friends at home.

> Please Dear Robert, remember us both to James Lynch, wife and family and not forgetting the old man. I hope that they are all well. I suppose Jim is in with Sarah yet and has a big family. Now please let me know did Dan Connell get married yet or is he lying alone yet? If he is, tell him to come out here, and that I will get some old winch for him here, that will have some money.

On that last light note, we may depart the North American scene.

Chapter Three

Fresh Frontiers: South Africa *circa* 1858-65

*The Government are opening a line of road from Georgesus Town
to Cafferland, a distance of 600 miles, right through the forest. The
part where I and my companions live was never trod by man
before. We have not a house within 40 miles of us. Still we feel
quite content in those parts [which] is frequented by wild animals
such as lions, bears, tigers, elephants and jackalls etc.* [1]

I

Having apparently spurned the chance of partaking in chain
migration to North America where at least two of his uncles had
settled, Christopher Miller *circa* 1858 struck out boldly on his
own account and headed off for South Africa. He left behind a
career in the Irish police force. In its stead he warmly embraced
a new-found situation soon after arrival at Simon's Bay near
Cape Town where he followed in the tracks of a pioneering
group of Irish colonists, who had initially stretched out South
African frontiers nearly forty years earlier.[2] From Simon's Bay
he wrote home to Coolybrown.

People at home may say that this country is very warm. It is
not the case. I felt a great deal hotter days at home than I felt
here. This climate is very healthy. I could sleep in the open
air at night and not get the slightest kind of sickness by so
doing. I truly wished that all my friends and relations were
out here and if Tobias was here he could do right well. I
have not wrote to him as I do not know where I should
direct my letter. I have wrote to Australia to James Winter
but got no answer. There is bad accounts from Australia here
lately.

At a few strokes of the pen, Christy Miller fills out the far-flung
nature of the Irish emigrants' field. Not alone could he have
opted for North America, he could also - notwithstanding the
recent bad reports - have gone to Australia, where his aunt
Thirza had settled along with her husband, James Winter.

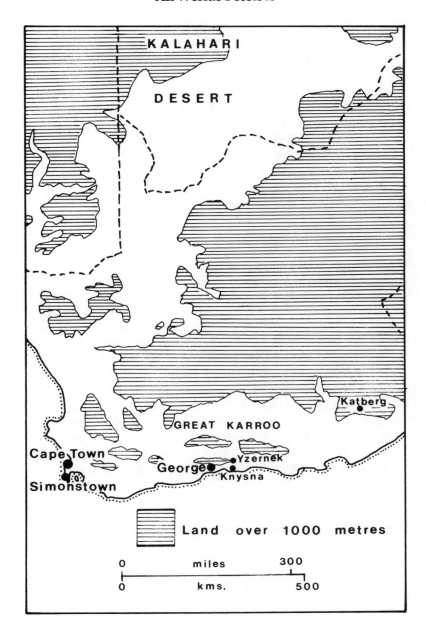

Fig. 7   Christopher Miller's South African sphere *circa* 1858-65

However, Christy was a man with an independent turn of mind and it shows when he sets himself up boldly in South Africa as the potential target of chain migration from home or from other emigrant spheres.

The recency of his own emigration shows too in his identity and familiarity with things at home and in his preliminary assessment of life and prices in South Africa.

> Dear Parents, I am glad to hear that your crops are fair this season and that your stock is good, and that the mare has a good foal. Do not think of selling that foal! —
>
> In general, they do not work hard here. Men must work a great [deal] harder at home and not half so well fed. Provisions in general are cheap with the exception of potatoes which sells at the rate of 1 lb. 3d. or lb. tea beats ten 2 shillings, or lb. shuggar 3d. per lb., Beef 4s.-8d. per lb., [and] mutton the same rate as beef. If a man wants to drink he can drink the best wine or brandy for 4d. per pint. As for my part, and you may depend on what I say, I do not taste one drop of any sort of intoxicating liquor whatever!

The passage cited here fits in well with a view of Irish emigrant correspondence which emphasises its consistent satisfied worldliness.[3] The pre-eminent concerns are with material things, especially prices and wages - a fixation that was perhaps natural enough among people whose relative poverty at home had yielded to relative affluence abroad. As well, Christy Miller brought in his own right the qualities of steadiness, decency, even outright abstemiousness, to illuminate his letters home.

He is a soberly religious man, thanking the Lord that he did not proceed to Australia in the ship in which he emigrated, since it went down in transit with the loss of 147 lives. He vows also that if the Lord spares him he will see his parents again before many years have elapsed. He is full of filial and fraternal feeling and he asks to be remembered at home to uncles, cousins, neighbours and friends.

> I now conclude by sending you, my ever dear parents, best love and also to my dear brothers Edward, Robert and Richard.
>
> Please dear Mamma, remember me to my dear uncles Jacob and family and to Robert, John Do[u]pe and uncle John in Kiltane, and not forgetting Thomas Healy and family, Michael Liston and family and all inquiring friends.

He expects a reply by return of post and asks that it be directed to Mr. Christopher Miller, Simon's Bay, at Melville's living stables, Cape of Good Hope, South Africa. Finally by way of a postscript to this undated fragment of a letter, he discloses that he had seen his master (Mr. Melville) only once in five months.

The nature of his work remains undisclosed. Indeed such scant evidence as is available comes by way of a note from his Cape Town employer, dated 7 July 1858, which refers in the first instance to the dismissal of an underling.

> Mr. Miller, you would have been perfectly right if you had discharged him on the spot. Therefore do so and I will get another in his place. You are doing all right, but do not let sailors have saddle horses or gig as there is a very great rush.

It appears as if Christy was in charge of the hire of horses in a port location, a situation that would fit in well with one of the family predilections, i. e. the great love of horses. Moreover, since he is eager to send on home his employer's correspondence with himself, Christopher Miller was in the time-honoured phrase 'doing well.'

II

The next available piece from Christy Miller is also undated and incomplete. Again judging from the content, it represents portion of an early letter written from in or about Cape Town. It is immediately revealing since it shows that even in distant South Africa there was scope to develop a Palatine sense of camaraderie.

> I am happy to have to tell you, my ever dear father and mother, that I met Mrs. Switzer in the Cape of Good [Hope]. She has been very kind to me and strongly advises me to stop in this country. She showed me some letters from her son and daughter from Australia and they are wishing to be back again to this colony. Mrs. Switzer is very well off. She has as splendid a house as Mr. Maunsell,[4] a large cloth shop in Long Street [5] in Cape Town, and she is doing well. She will do what she can for me too, but thank God I want nothing from her. This is a country where Jack is as good as his master — Short that I am in this country if I wished I

> could get from any man who I would hire with £100 in cash
> — They would be shure to let me remain with them. The
> people of this country feel happy to have a white man live
> with them. A man that will take care of himself need not be
> in want of anything in this world here.

The friendship is welcome and the advice well taken. The
assessments are sensible and, as ever with Christopher Miller,
the pre-occupation is with material things. In what has been
referred to as the 'clean laboratories' of exile,[6] the innate
characteristics of the Irish Palatine community travelled well
and fitted in well with a transposed sense of Irishness abroad.

Christy Miller is a keen observer and also a cautious one.

> In my next letter as I told you before, I will be better able to
> give ye a more satisfactory account of the manner and
> customs of this country. The languages that is spoken here
> are Dutch and English. The religion[s] here are all
> Protestants, both Dutch and English. There are four sects of
> people here. First are the Malay race, 2nd the Hottentots, 3rd
> the Moors and 4th the Caffers. These sects are all black and
> in general very lazy and Paley?

The man from Coolybrown captures well the duality of ethnic
composition that underpinned South African colonialism,
together with its leading cultural characteristics. He also
adumbrates in the mode of the time the subservient classes, of
which the Hottentots and the Caffers may be seen as indigenous
and the Malays and the Moors as introduced elements to the
Cape colony. Again in the mode of the time, he writes off all
four ethnic groups as 'black', despite a considerable actual range
in the pigmentation of their skins and, as was customary for a
whiteman of his time, he characterises them in the usual
stereotypical way.

> Turning to another theme, Christy draws in the wider ambit of
the familial emigrant field and the connections with home,
including from himself the promise of a remittance. He is hard-
headed and pragmatic. There is nothing of the lachrymose
Irishman in exile here.

> I hope, dear parents, that ye have heard from Tobias before
> this time. For if I knew where to write to him I would send
> for him, for he could do right well here. I wished that ye all
> were out here— It is then I would be happy.

> Dear Parents, I hope in a short time to send you some

money with God['s] help, as I can very well afford it in a
short time. If the Lord spares me any health I will not forget
ye.

He ends by asking that the letter in reply should be sent c/o Mrs
Switzer in Cape Town. Clearly he was a man then on the move.
However, the matter of a forwarding address should be sorted
out by his next visit to town, from where Mrs. Switzer would re-
direct any incoming letters to him. He promises to keep in close
touch with home.

III

By the time of Christy Miller's next surviving letter to
Coolybrown, he had changed his employment and professed
himself well pleased with the change. This was on 10 May 1859
when he penned a long piece home, while using as an address
the Knysna Main Station in the Cape of Good Hope (fig. 7). His
former employer was sorry to lose him.

Mr. Melville felt very much at my leaving him. No man
could get a better discharge than he gave to me , which I
would send you, but fearing I might want it. He also made
me a present of £11-00 sterling and the best horse he had in
his possession, with bridle and saddle, and told me never to
want a friend while I knew where to find him.

The testimonial is obviously glowing. Christy Miller passed
with distinction his first test of individual worth on foreign soil.

However, it was his new employment which now held his
attention and he waxes enthusiastically about it.

My ever dear parents and brothers, I take this opportunity
to let ye know that I am well and I trust the Lord to find you
all in the same. I have changed my last employment by
getting a first rate situation. I got into government lodgings
and everything found. I can live quite at my ease. The
employment I am on is [a] permanent one and is considered
the best in Africa. The government are opening a line of
road from Georgesus Town[7] to Cafferland,[8] a distance of 600
miles, right through the forest. The part where I and my
companions live was never trod by man before. We have
not a house within 40 miles of us. Still we feel quite content
in those parts [which] is frequented by wild animals such as

Plate 7 The road 'right through the forest' to Avontuur via Yzernek

> lions, bears, tigers, elephants and jackalls etc. Now this road
> that I speak of is to be made by the convicts —- The
> prisoners here are all Blacks, Fingooses,[9] Caffers[10] and
> Hottentots,[11] who are guarded while at work by police and
> military — I am full overseer and about 4 hours per day
> finishes my day's work, and some days I have got nothing to
> do. And taking everything into consideration, the salary I
> now have, although £34 less than my former situation is far
> better, which I will shew you. First, my support and next
> my clothing which the government supply, and nothing to
> do. Secondly, if I am sick my pay goes on the same and [we]
> have a doctor to attend us. Thirdly, a fair prospect of rising
> very soon.

Christy Miller was well satisfied with his lot and as a welcome
throwback to the old days when he was assistant overseer to
Denis Hogan on the Kilscannell and Clounagh new lines he
writes: 'Now I derive a benefit from old Hogan's lectures on
road making.'

By virtue of his pioneering role, Christy was in a superb
position to offer insights into this vast world in the process of
being tamed by imperialism. He was a participant observer
right in the van of frontier making. Not only that, but he also
offers us a version of frontier hypothesis long before the

celebrated Frederick Jackson Turner invented one of his own.[12] Something much more profound than an American story has been adduced from Turner's oft quoted sentence:

> Stand at Cumberland Gap and watch the procession of civilisation, marching single file - the buffalo following the trail to salt springs, the Indian, the fur trader and hunter, the cattle raiser, the pioneer farmer.[13]

Equally something far more than an African story may be adduced from Miller's prosaic but no less compelling view of sequent occupance in Kaffraria:

> Now I will state as far as I know how the English acts in this part. First goes the army with the sword [and] sweeps the country before them. Next comes the missionary and settles himself in the best part where he will become rich. Next the magistrate and takes command of a district and settles himself as happy as a king. Next comes the surveyor with his chain and divides the spoil as he calculates best and so forth.

The man from Coolybrown had plugged into one of the most vital and energising themes in South African historiography[14] and had done so with the benefit of a shrewd eye and a discerning mind.

By this stage, however, he is much more equivocal about the prospect of migration to South Africa. This is couched both in general terms and specifically in the case of a prospective emigrant from Ireland.

> Any person who intends to come to this country must make up his mind to rough all that comes before him, but thanks be to God, since placing my foot on Africa I never knew what a day's work was. But one thing I have to say, it is not every person was so well able to work out their point — I received that note from Henry Crawford. And with respect to him sending out his son I really cannot advise him, for where he would have to land to where I am is a distance of 800 miles and I know that he could not take part in the same employment —- As for farming, no man from the old country has the least idea of how farming is carried on here. If a man intends to work, let him work at home. In this country no white men work or if they do it is their own fault. But parties who come out on free emigration are well provided for after they land. There is a depot formed by

government and they can remain there gratius till such time
as they are employed. I would advise any person who can
find a situation or employment at home to remain and not
travel. It is not every constitution that is able to stand an
African sun or the hot winds which during the time it lasts
[one is] not able to breathe. But thanks be to God I never
enjoyed better health than since I left home. [I] never got the
slightest change.

Tempered no doubt by his experience of frontier living,
Christy's appraisal of South Africa as a potential emigrant field
was suitably modified. His attitude to work on the other hand
typified that of the frontiersman, who regarded the non-white
only as a servant or an enemy.[15] As much as anything, the term
'Kaffir work' is a measure of the whiteman's disdain for the
labouring classes.

Changing direction, and attuning himself to home and the
wider familial and neighbourhood setting, he firstly engages his
mother, then both parents, and finally his mother again.

Dear Mother, I received your letter on the 5th May and
nothing in the world can give me greater comfort, also
hearing from my brother Tobias that he was doing well was
most pleasing news and I request of you if he writes to send
his letter to me. I feel thankful to Almighty God that it had
pleased [Him] to raise up my dear father and brothers from
a bed of sickness on[ce] more and I trust in his mercy that
this will find ye all as well as I am at present. Dear Parents,
do not blame me for not sending ye some money now. I
never was better able. I am master of £50.00 sterling, but
where I am is 200 miles to Georgeus Town where I could get
an order. But rely on me. The first time I go there with
God['s] help I shall send something worth while. —
Dear Mother, if the Lord spares [me] for ten years I will
shurely return home,independent for life and give over
travelling.

By way of a postscript, he testifies once again to his status of
frontiersman by mentioning the enclosure of a Caffer chief's
gown, who had been taken prisoner and had gotten twelve
months confinement. He asks for the very same set of uncles,
cousins and neighbours as before, and perhaps with a view to
helping out or simply satisfying his curiosity, he seeks that in
'your next letter, dear Mamma, you will let me know how you

are all situated in circumstance.' As for himself, he has cause to
be thankful in being so fortunate, but he adds cryptically ' not
forever.'

IV

By the time of Christy's next extant letter, it is clear that he held
on resolutely to his post as road overseer on a projected route
from George to British Kaffraria. This was in November 1862,
when he wrote home from Yzernek.

Plate 8   Looking down over the great loop of the road snaking through
          Yzernek ('the iron pass')

My ever dear parents and brothers, I take this favourable
opportunity to write these few lines, still thrusting in the
Almighty to find you all well and doing well, as I am at
present. I am still in the same situation and do not intend to
leave it for some time. My salary is £50 per annum and
found in the following rations daily:$1^1/_2$ lb. bread, $1^1/_2$ lb.
meat, 2 oz. tea, $^1/_2$ oz. salt, together with quarters and a
servant, and not [the] least kind of hardship.

In his view no employment is as sure as government work. He
accounts it the best in health and in sickness and he has no

notion of forsaking it, while continuing to reside 'in this part of the globe.' He goes on to assuage his mother's concerns about religious observance.

> Dear mother, you wish to know our place of worship. We have on the station the English Church where service is every morning, and on Sunday morning and evening, and no matter what sect or creed a man belongs to on this establishment he must attend at church at the hours appointed.

As he had set out earlier in his own version of sequent occupance, the Church followed directly upon the army in pioneering the settlement frontier.[16]

In other respects, however, things had changed radically by the time Christy penned this letter on 13 November 1862. In particular, the impact of the American Civil War was deep and negative.

> As this colony is at present, the people are in a state of starvation. Provisions rate at famine prices which is as follows: 180 lbs flour, £7-10, meat 9s. per lb., butter 2 shillings per lb., potatoes 4d. per lb. [There is] no employment. The labouring class[es] [are] very badly off and every person who is able to leave is emigrating to New Zealand as the passage from here is low and I would strongly advise any person who thinks of emigration to try some other part. For whoever comes here will repent it to their heart's content — It is true that there is plenty of land, yes, and fit for all kinds of cultivation. No country better. But poor people when they land here, perhaps not the second pound sterling in their pocket, with large families, how are they able to commence farming. And on the other hand, land sells very high. The Dutch farmers in general depend on stock and scarcely rear provisions for their [own] use, and generally speaking both English and Irish farmers follow the same example. The American war has injured the country very much at present, but I think and have others' opinions, that it will serve it in the co[u]rse of a few years as more cultivation has taken place this year than since the slaves was emancipated.

It took from *circa* 1860 to *circa* 1914 to close the agricultural and pastoral frontier. All the while, the world of pastoralism as identified in the farming practices of the Dutch, the English and

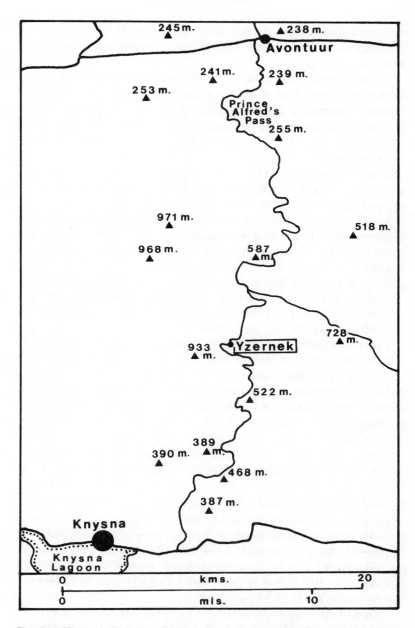

Fig. 8   The road through Yzernek ('the iron pass') to Avontuur
overseen by Christopher Miller *circa* 1859-64

the Irish kept its clear ascendancy, while the cultivated area increased more than twenty fold to reach almost seven million acres.[17]

Finally Christy focuses upon home and the extended family domain and, as ever, is anxious for news of family, relations and friends. Perhaps a bit of gossip would not go amiss. He complains, in any event, of his mother's parsimony with the news.

> Dear mother, in your last letter [you] never let me know how ye were situated or doing. You merely mentioned that it had been a very wet season, but never told me any other family matters. I hope in answer to this that you will let me know all particulars, or if anything interesting has taken place, or if there is any account from Tobias, or from Australia. —
>
> I desire to be kindly remembered to all my dear relations both in Killeheen, Court[matrix] and Kyletaun and to my dear uncle Robert in Adare, and tell him that I shall write to him soon. Give my best respects to Michael Liston and family and all inquiring friends.
>
> I now conclude. May the Almighty God bless and preserve you, my ever dear parents and brothers, is the sincere wish of your affectionate son.

Ever the dutiful son, Christopher Miller kept in close touch with home. The only missing element is actual inclusion rather than just the promise of remittances.

V

Appropriately for a man who had spent years in the van of a frontier drive, the last of Christy Miller's extant letters comes from hard by the boundary of British colonial possessions in Southern Africa. The man from Coolybrown had made the traverse from core to outer periphery, from Cape Town to Katberg (fig. 7). And it is from the convict station in Katberg that he writes home on 11 July 1865.

> Since the date of my last letter I have been transferred to the above named place, still in the same employment, with a slight increase in pay. From Yzernek to this place is a distance of 600 miles in the interior. You will see by the map

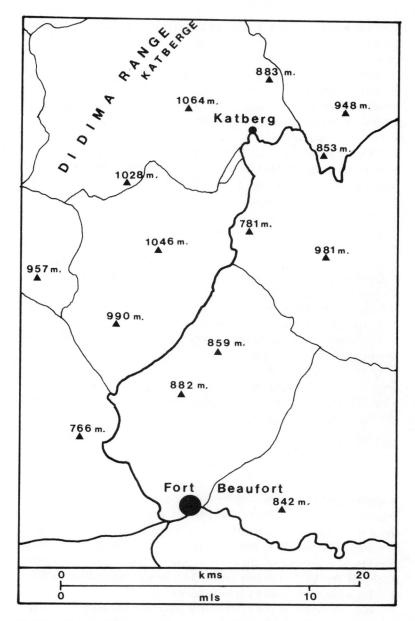

Fig. 9 The road leading from Fort Beaufort northwards through the Katberg Pass where Christopher Miller was overseer in 1865

of this country that Katberg in the division of Stockmstrom is near the farthest point that the English possessions reach and close by the Great Basuto Chief Mozshes, who is a friendly chief and embraces the white man and is a sincere Christian and member of the established Church of England.

Here Christy Miller touches on a theme whereby British colonial interests stretched across boundaries and coerced or cajoled chiefs and their tribesmen into submission and/or conformity. The process was actively under way beyond the Kat River settlement in the 1840s and 50s,[18] and by 1865 the measure of its success is clear in the case of the great Basuto chief.

Plate 9   The top of the Katberg Pass

Turning to the broad theme of emigration, Christy brings to bear on the subject his own steadiness, decency and good sense. He also holds out for any white emigrant the promise of equality and fraternity, qualities which are decisively lacking in Ireland.

Dear Mother, I wish to let you know that a man who respects and takes care in a respectful manner will be respected and never want for anything. People in this country or any country where there is emigration to are far different in their manners to what they are at home. We look on each other as friends and relations, not as strangers, for

> we are all strangers in a strange land. So every white person whom we meet will or must assist each other, no matter of what sect or creed.

No doubt word of Christy's sentiments spread to friends and relations in Killeheen, Courtmatrix, Kyletaun and Adare, as well as the neighbourhood of Coolybrown, and helped to perpetuate the chain of long distance migration.

The other major theme that he dwells upon is the sense of shared sorrow that binds a family, no matter how scattered, after the loss of a loved member. In this case it was Christy's brother Tobias, who at the age of thirty-nine had died in America. He asks for all at home, being puzzled as to why there was no mention of his brother Robert in the last two letters he had received, and again there is the promise rather than the delivery of a remittance.

> I will send to my father what I have promised. He will get it an[d] no mistake.

There is also the promise of his returning home for a short time by April 1866. However, the thought of living for good in a land racked by landlord oppression would cause him to entertain thoughts of suicide. On the other hand, bring the most superior of the landlord class to South Africa and they would be no better than any other person.

There is no evidence that Christy ever came home. Rather, he appears to have lived out his life in South Africa, and the only other occasion in which he figures in the extant Miller correspondence is when his brother Richard asks for him, when writing home from India in June 1879. By that time, this pioneering frontiersman who had earlier traversed the spectrum of colonial interests in his chosen sphere, would have been 51 years of age.

Chapter Four

Service Abroad : India 1869-79

*I am quite content with a happy single life and as I have roamed
for ten years through the burning sun of India, I think I might be
able to roam another ten through this world if the Lord spares me,
without seeking a wife. I dare say I could have got an Indian bride
long before this far.*[1]

I

Following on from the mutiny of the Indian army in 1857 and its
successful suppression, British imperial interests took over the
direct rule of the sub-continent, and as ever in such situations,
primary significance attached to the imperial army in enforcing
and monitoring rule. Such are the circumstances that set the
broad context for Richard Miller's stint abroad soon after
enlisting in the 62nd Regiment Foot at the Castle Barracks,
Limerick in September 1868. From the first of his surviving
letters home, we find Richard serving at Lucknow, the old
Mogul city, located in the great sweep of the Upper Gangetic
Plains (fig. 10). Along with Delhi, Lucknow had been the
decisive location in turning the scale of events in 1857,[2] and thus
its strategic value in the grand imperial design may be readily
appreciated.

However, none of this bothered Richard Miller when penning
a short letter to his brother Edward at Coolybrown, on 19
August 1872. His concerns were direct and immediate, and
pertained to the spread of contagious disease of pandemic
proportions.

My dear Brother, I write you these few lines hoping this will
find you in the enjoyment of good health, as this leaves me
at present. I thank God for his kind mercies. Dear Brother,
my reason for writing is all over this country is one mass of
sickness, raging cholera, Dingue? fever. The fever disease is
raging very badly in Lucknow at the present time and the
latter has just made its appearance.

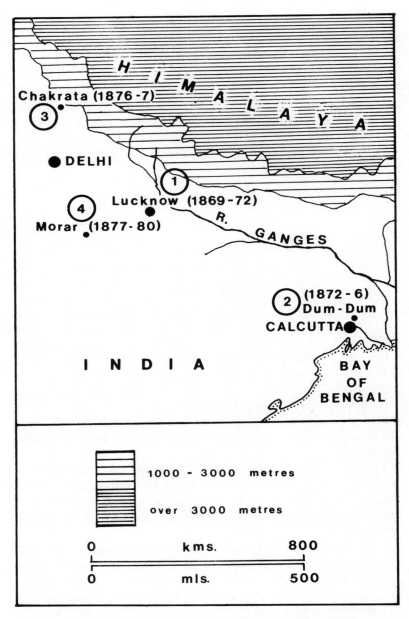

Fig. 10   Richard Miller's record of army service in India, 1869-79

But our regiment is enjoying the best of health thank God.
I have no account from ? Delmege lately. I shall write to
[him] on the 20th. The rains are very heavy here at present.
I hope father and mother and Robert are enjoying good
health and all uncles, aunts and cousins and all inquiring
friends, is the sincere wish of your affectionate brother,
R. Miller.

He asks by way of postscript that his writing be excused, 'for it
was in hast[e],' and also that a reply be directed 'as usual.'
Nevertheless this short perfunctory note sets the tone of
Richard's epistolary pieces and marks him out as by far the least
forthcoming of the Miller brothers.

And he had much to be forthcoming about. For instance,
there was the burst of the Monsoon which he dismisses in a
sentence, or the cultural and geographical setting of Lucknow,
to which he fails to advert altogether. He has nothing to say of
this Mogul centre built on the sordid exploitation of the peasant
masses, or of its ' clumsy and garish provincialism — the
bastard progeny of debased Oriental and debased European
models ' reflecting ' an appalling decadence.'[3] But if Richard
Miller leaves a cold trail in describing and evaluating Lucknow,
then most assuredly Oskar Spate, the greatest geographer of
India to write in English, warms to the task.

Buildings, which look like marble by moonlight, are shown
by the disillusioning sun to be degraded examples of stucco
and brick. Flying buttresses to support nothing but one
another, copper domes gilt from top to bottom, burnished
umbrellas and balustrades of baked clay form a gallery of
architectural horror perhaps matched only in the Indo-
British buildings of Bombay.[4]

Spate, the geographer, captures well the depravity of the
Nawabs of Oudh in terms of the grossness and excesses of their
urban creation. Miller, the soldier, conveys nothing at all of it.

II

By the time of Richard Miller's next surviving communication,
he and his regiment had moved camp to Chakrata. Here in the
shadow of the Siwalik Range, they were still located in the
Upper Gangetic Plains, some 400 miles north west of Lucknow

and some 150 miles due north of Delhi (fig. 10). As before, Miller fails to furnish the least detail of his intriguing sub-Siwalik setting where the stream profiles suddenly flatten out and the coarser detritus, consisting of boulders and gravels, is deposited to yield a great detrital piedmont known as the *bhabar* (='porous').[5] However, on the plus side, three of Richard's surviving letters written in the period April-October 1877 and all addressed from Chakrata, emanated from this distinctive sub-montane setting in northern India.

The first, dated 2 April 1877, is addressed to his brother, Edward, shortly after their brother Robert had brought in a wife to the homeplace at Coolybrown. As usual, the concerns are mundane, personal, familial.

> Dear Brother, I received your kind and welcome letter, finding me in the enjoyment of good health. Hoping this will find you all in the same state, thank God. I received the ribbon alright. The one you sent before this — is nearly worn out and we can hardly get anything where we are stationed for the present. You can tell my brother Robert that I wishes him joy and [I am] very glad to hear that I have got a sister, which I should like for them to send this likeness.

The only thing of Chakrata that emerges is its backwardness, relative isolation, and dearth of retail and service outlets.

Asked as to how India in general agrees with him, Richard is curt, ungracious and unforthcoming. In this and in other ways he appears, as by far the youngest member of the family, to have carried something of the spoilt child syndrome with him into adulthood.

> You asked me to let you know how the country is agreeing with me. I am enjoying very good health for the present and for I to say anything about India, I should be stating a falsehood.

To follow on, he will only allow that if anyone wants to know about India they had better come and experience it, just as he was obliged to do himself. Then with a sting of bitterness in the tail, he points to the push of migration away from a homeland that had failed miserably to sustain him.

The same kind of niggardliness is apparent in his final passage where, beginning with his brother Edward's impending emigration to Australia, he flits from one topic to another in rapid succession.

> Let me know when you leave for Australia. I also have got another rise to color sergeant since I last wrote. I hope mother is enjoying good health as I expect to see her once more and the place of my birth, if the Lord spares me to return home once more. Let me know is there any account from the Delmeges as I hear nothing about them in any of your letters —
>
> Remember me to uncle John Doupe[6] and cousins, [and] to aunt Eliza and uncle Jacob and cousins. Give them my best respects and to all enquiring friends, is the sincere wish of your affectionate brother, Richard Miller.

For a postscript he adds with a flourish his serial number and rank, and the address at which he can be reached: No. 1462, Color Sergeant Richard Miller, Letter F Company, HM 62 Regiment, Chakrata, East India.

The second of Richard Miller's letters from Chakrata, dated 29 June 1877, is addressed to his brother Robert at Coolybrown. Edward's heralded departure to Australia had by then become a reality, and so out of five sons who survived into adulthood, only one remained at home. The familial order had moved on to the next generation with all of its concomitant changes; the old matriarch was in decline.

> Very sorry to hear that mother was enjoying such bad health, as my brother Edward never stated to me in all his letters and I was very sorry to hear that you and him could not agree by your letter which you wrote to me. And now he is gone to Australia which you stated to me, as he told me that he was going. When I get an account from him, I shall let you know, as he promised to write to me as soon as he landed there.

The network of family interconnection by way of letters would tie together Ireland, India and Australia, and serve to mitigate the pain of separation. As a leading analyst of emigrant correspondence writes, 'the acts of composing, sending, awaiting, receiving and reading letters were important symbols of contact.'[7] Letters were also re-directed and re-read. Indeed, such was the ritual of communication that emigrant correspondence assumed the character of an institution.

Almost invariably too, questions were put and thoughts entertained about returning home, whether for a visit or for good. As Richard wrote in response to Robert's prompting:

> Dear Brother, you ask me about my coming home. This is a
> question I cannot answer for the present as we leave about
> November for Morar on the plains again, so that I think we
> shall leave for England about 1880. But before I leave
> Chakrata I shall ? a Cashmere shawl. I would send one at
> the present time but I cannot get none to suit me.

He then refers to the enclosure of a photograph of himself, sent
as a token of fellowship, before again re-visiting his mother with
his best wishes.

> I enclose my likeness with this letter as a love for you all.
> Still hoping she might look more at this than the other ones I
> sent home as a mere emblem of my native place. Still
> hoping mother is getting strong and may the Lord protect all
> our excellent universe.

He concludes with the wish of 'every joy, peace and happiness'
for those at home and he adds by way of postscript a reminder
to send a length of three or four yards of black ribbon for his
cape, and a reply by return regarding his mother's health.

The last of Richard's letters from Chakrata, dated 15 October
1877, was also destined for his brother Robert at Coolybrown.
Straightaway after the usual epistolary opening, there is concern
over their failing mother's health, followed by evidence of
discordance between the brothers Robert and Edward over the
recent parting of their ways.

> I was very sorry to hear that mother is enjoying bad health. I
> had a letter a few days ago from Edward which I enclose.
> But I have not complied with his request as to send him your
> last letter. I am not so simple.

Continuing, he refers to the ribbon that he had requested in his
last letter. Such enclosures tended to give anxiety to both
senders and recipients,[8] and as was the case here, advice was
tendered as to the correct means of postage (1) for the ribbon
that had been returned to sender and (2) for a soldier's watch
yet to be forwarded.

> The ribbon, you should have sent it as packet post or parcel
> post, and it would not have been returned. As you say,
> you are going into Limerick after this winter. You might
> buy me one of those soldier's watches. You will get it quite
> cheap. In any way, send it by parcel post and register it. I
> am going to send home a shawl for a Christmas box. I am

> going to send it next month. We leave this station on the 3rd
> December next for Morar. To go to there [is] a distance of
> about 800 miles which will come very expensive upon me. I
> hope I shall receive the ribbon before you get this.

Richard was a great man for tokens, looking to receive as well as
to give, while scrupulously managing to avoid any mention of
an emigrant's remittance.

As to the prospect of his coming home, he responds in the
same vein as before.

> This is a question that I could not answer for the present. It
> might be next year or it might be in a couple of years, if the
> Lord spares me my health.

Then in his usual brusque manner he adds, ' I have not much to
say at present.' He sends his usual regards and the only
fragment that he divulges of his life as a soldier in Chakrata is
being then on guard. Ever demanding, he seeks an answer by
return of post, and to conclude he issues a caution: 'Let not a
particle of Edward's letter be known to anyone outside of
doors.'

III

Having left for Morar in December 1877, Richard Miller's next
available letter comes from there, but not until 1 June 1879. As
he signalled in an earlier communication, Morar belongs too to
the Upper Gangetic Plains, being located some 200 miles WSW
of Lucknow and almost due south of the famous Mogul city of
Agra. It was a most unprepossessing place. Richard Miller
places it in the 'Maharajah of Reindias' and accounts it ' one of
the worst stations of India.' No doubt at the time of writing, his
temper was severely influenced by the build-up of pre-Monsoon
heat and humidity.[9] As he put it: 'We are almost wasted with
the heat this year.' In response, they were obliged to operate the
ventilation system day and night, in order to keep the barracks
cool.

Nor does Richard's temper appear to have been mollified
through his brother Robert's teasing about the girls back home.

> Dear Brother, I think you are taking a rise out [of] me about
> the Kiltane and Killeheen girls, that I need not dread about
> getting a lady when I come home. Yes, they can remain as
> they are, for all I care. I am quite content with a happy

Station, Garrison, Barrack, General Hospital, &c.	Date of arrival at the Station	No. in Admission and Discharge Book	Date of						Diseases. (a) Primary (b) Secondary	Duration of Diseases Days
			Admission to Hospital			Discharge from Hospital				
			Year	Mo.	Day	Year	Mo.	Day		
Cork	Sept/68	Landed in India 2.2.69								
Lucknow	24/2/69	195	69	4	15	69	4	22	Diarrhoea	7
"		223	"	4	22	"	5	4	Pneumonia	11
		982	"	10	10	"	10	24	Diarrhoea	23
Dum Dum	7.12.72	676	72	12	10	72	12	16	Diarrhoea	7
Chakrata	20. 2. 76									
Morar	25/12/77	1161	79	11	10	79	11	18	Ague	3
"	"	1344	79	12	6	80	1	4	Bronchitis	29
"	"	16	80	1	4	80	1	20	Pneumonia	16
"	"	645	80	6	24	80	7	31	S C Fever	38
"	"	857	80	8	17				Ague	

Plate 10 Constructing Richard Miller's Indian sphere from his medical history

single life and as I have roamed for ten years through the burning sun of India I think I might be able to roam another ten through this world if the Lord spares me, without seeking a wife. I dare say I could have got an Indian bride long before this far. I could not evil myself.

The Miller predilection for the single life is well exemplified here. Richard was then aged thirty-one and like his brothers, Christopher in South Africa and Edward in Australia, he seemed set fair to eschew the matrimonial state.[10] Still for all that, he asks to be remembered to 'all friends and young maids in Coolybrown and adjoinings.'

Flitting from one topic to another in the concluding passage, Richard begins with a deep expression of sorrow about his ailing mother, while still harbouring the hope that he would see her once more before she died. That chance never came, as she was to pass on to the 'realms of Joy' later in the same month. Richard then inquires if there is any account from Christopher or from America and asks that his warmest regards be conveyed to his aunts, uncles and cousins in Kiltane, Killeheen and Court[matrix].[11] He singles out uncle John Doupe, whom he hopes to meet soon again to get forgiveness for storming out of the Doupe house, just before joining the army. Lastly, there is the conveyance of best love for mother, Annie and baby - three female figures spanning the spectrum of family life, while also symbolising the changing familial order at home in Coolybrown.

After that, there is no more from the pen of this serving soldier on the plains of India. Indeed, his only subsequent appearance in the Miller papers comes by way of his brother, Edward, from Australia. This was in a letter of 8 November 1881, and it shows Richard in anything but a flattering light.

> I got no other letter since from Dick —– He ought to be ashamed of himself to ask money of me. I heard he asked a certain young lady in the Co. of Limerick to become his wife or something to that purpose —– Even a fool can make money but it takes a wise man to keep it.

If it was the case that Richard had fallen into dissolute ways, then he was singularly on his own among the Miller brotherhood of Coolybrown.[12] One thing at least is certain: he marched to the beat of a different drum to any of the rest of them.

Chapter Five

Traversing the Outback : Australia *circa* 1855-93

The country is cleared for a few miles about Melbourne, but up the country tis nothing but bush or scrub and trees, and the country is nothing but a wilderness and lonely place. The settlers are very few. In the places that I passed through in fact you will not see the face of a Christian for days and weeks.[1]

I

In order of chronology, the earliest letters from Australia to find a destination or resting place in Coolybrown come from the pen of James Winter, the brother-in-law of Barbara Miller. Taking them in probable sequence, the first is addressed to Winter's brother, John, whom we later learn had connections through marriage with Reens near Coolybrown; the second is to Barbara herself; while the third, and only one to be dated and complete on all accounts, is to Winter's nephew, Edward Miller.

Judging from the context provided by the first two letters, James Winter and his wife Thirza, whom he married in 1836, appear to have been caught up in the great sweep of post-Famine emigration from Ireland. They were, in any event, in Australia before 1858 [2] and clearly in good time to participate in the great gold rushes of the 1850s and 60s.[3] The allurements of gold feature prominently in James' letter from Springs, Melbourne to his brother John, for whom, it appears, remittances were being gathered among the transposed Winter family, to enable him too to come to Australia.

Dear Brother, I am in good health. I expected to hear from the boys, as they promised to send me some money for to send you along, with whatever I could spare myself. But they never wrote to me since they went up the country. I spent only eleven weeks in a stranger's employment since I came out. I took one tour to the diggings last October and stopped out, between travelling and working for ten weeks.

I made £111-2-4 of what got picked up. The people have made fortunes now by gold digging. This country is full of gold. In some places they pick it up as fast as you might pick pebbles on the square of Dromcoloher. They dig from one foot to 30 or 40 feet deep. When I worked I knew a party of men in 2 months to get 197 lbs. weight of gold. A man pick'd out of a sod a wedge of gold worth £180. A man may earn £3 per day. The fact is wherever you turn your face is a gold field.

James Winter was from the Dromcolliher area of west Limerick and his metaphor relating to the town square is an entrancing one. It is reminiscent of a Percy French song, but not the one that French penned about Dromcolliher. However, in reality everything about the gold rushes and the fever these engendered, was ephemeral. The ubiquity of gold, as signalled in Winter's last sentence, was always going to prove illusory. Still, reportage of the vintage cited here, must have acted as a powerful psychological inducement for many at home to head off for far Australia.

And the implications are all the more easily understood when Winter turns back to focus on Ireland. Family and countrymen are tied in to, what for them, is a land of want.

I send you a draft for £10. It is only a present. I hope you wont think it too small. Dear John, there is nothing to trouble me but home, when I think of my poor countrymen working hard for Indian meal and to see the bullocks heads left in the field to the dogs. You will tell my poor mother if she still lives she may have plenty of money between the boys and me. I do not wish to drain myself out, as I have no home yet. It is living with Edward I am and I intend to fix a living when I will be my own landlord. But not a word about Tirzah nor any of the family.

The letter then stops abruptly. The rest is missing. Still enough is intact to enable us to place it in the heyday of the gold strikes of the 1850s in an Australian context. As for Ireland, we can place it in the context of the travail caused by the Great Famine.

The second of James Winter's letters to his sister-in-law, Barbara Miller, is also undated and lacks a home address. However, like the first, it belongs to the Winters' early colonising days in Australia. In the opening passage there is reference to unhappy pre-emigration days at home and also a need to sort out some family misunderstandings that may have arisen both at home and in Australia.

My Dr. Sister Barbara, You can plainly see that I am not the writer of your sister's[4] letter which was my bounden duty not on her account alone but on yours also. And I think it right to state the cause which is plainly this: In the first place when I took pen and paper to write, I first read your former letter and though far away I am, I read with tears. [I] was obliged to withdraw and when I came in to my tent, I requested of one of my mates to write for me. Now after an hour's composure I take the liberty of trespassing on your time. Hoping that you entertain the same opinion of me as you did on our first acquaintance, and be convinced my Dr. Barbara that I never for one moment lost my least esteem for you, although I did not go to see you. I think you will be the more ready to admit this when you recollect the untoward circumstances I was placed in for some time before I left home. But the Lord be praised for his mercies.

Plainly there was reconciliation to be made, and James Winter set about the task of trying to clear up outstanding differences with his sister-in-law.

Following on from these strictly family matters, the same kind of rugged materialism that underpins so much of Irish emigrant correspondence from Australia[5] is given full vent by James Winter.

Either me nor my wife never knew want since we came to this country. We have the best preserves [of] all kinds that England can produce [and] Irish bacon and butter, as well as our colonial produce. Dr. B, your sister never had reason to buy a stone of sugar or flour, nor a pound of tea, as the first supply of tea I put in the tent where I now sit to write this rigmarole was 140 lbs., with a similar complement of sugar, first quality flour, bacon, butter, pickles, jams etc. etc. Besides we have about 20 laying hens and when Tirzah can spare a dozen of fresh eggs she can get from 9s. (45p.) to 12s. (60p.) per dozen for them. I knew fresh eggs to fetch 2s./6 d. (12$\frac{1}{2}$ p.) each here. Besides this, I have fenced a piece of ground and cultivated it in such a manner as that I had radishes, turnips, onions, shillotts in abundance for the whole season and I am sure if I counted what cabbage and lettuce together with a little of the aforesaid that it would exceed £50. And my Dr. Barbara, Believe me I done all this besides working with my mates at gold digging, that is to say by over hours and sometimes by moonlight. I leave you now to guess whether I work hard or not. I have two mates who board with me and one of which wrote Thirzah's letter. He is Captain FitzHerbert, late of the Horse Guards.

Winter thus furnishes convincing evidence of material well being on the part of himself and his wife, and he also clears up the authorship of the disputed letter with which he started off his own epistolary address to Barbara.

He then concludes, and in the process furnishes a significant clue.

Tell sister Rebecca that I intend to write her that sencible letter but the pick and shovel has spoiled my penmanship and the blythe and salt sweat has w[e]akened my light. But yet I hope to see and you far to[o] far — Believe me to be your most affectionate brother till death.

Mention of Rebecca who was married to John Doupe of Courtmatrix means that the letter pre-dated April 1856, because Rebecca died at that time. Also it is clear that the letter belongs to a very early phase of colonisation, given the apparent lack of a permanent abode and the apparent paucity of Australian idiom that intruded into the writer's consciousness.[6] Indeed, given the weight of circumstantial evidence, it is probably fair to place the letter in the early-to-mid 1850s.

No ambiguity whatever attends the third of James Winter's letters. This is from Wedderburn in Victoria (fig. 11), it is dated 10 April 1877, and it is addressed to Edward Miller at Coolybrown. Emigration was then to the fore of Edward's mind, and like his brother Christopher at a much earlier date, he was taking soundings from a relative abroad.

My Dr Nephew, We recd. your letter on the 6th Inst. and are glad to hear the few friends you mentioned are well, as we are at the time of writing this. The Lord be praised for his mercies. You want my advice as to whether this or America would be the likeliest place for a young man to get a living. With regard to this country, gold digging is not a payable pursuit for many years past, but as you say you have capital. You can go and travel the country as far as you please and select any area not exceeding 320 acres of land, which is the highest one person can get. But each person in a family can

get the same amt., if they have the means to comply with the
regulations of the clauses of the Land Act. As to state the
clauses in full I cannot, but this I know that when you select,
you have to send notice of the same and at the first land
board held in the district your case will be recommended or
rejected. You will have to pay for the survey before you
enter on the land and then make certain improvements and
pay a rent of 2/0 (10p.) per acre per annum for 10 years, and
then you get your crown grant as fee simple estate. There
are six [of] my nephews [who] have selected within 7 miles
of this place and each holding the largest area allowed. And
I thank my God they are all located on one square block
adjoining each other. As the Lord placed the children of
Israel in the land of Canaan, so he has placed my friends in
this good land. I would say there is good land in the same
locality not taken up yet. It is heavily timbered, the
grubbing and clearing of which will cost about £2 per acre.

The sentiments are almost identical in tenor with those
addressed to Christopher Miller by his Canadian uncle some
twenty-five years earlier. Whatever about the occasional
allurements of gold now that the heyday of the strikes had
passed, the land of Australia was held out as a prize there for
the taking by someone inured to a life of farming at home. And
it was a prize worth the taking as evidenced by Winter's
masterly portrayal of chain migration on the ground as stage-
managed by the divine ordering of the Lord. The grapevine
operated by kin had also something quite profound to do with
it.[7]

To finish, Winter pursues a general thematic line on Australia
with particular emphasis on climate, which as we have already
seen, was often a pre-occupation of the distant migrant out of
Ireland.

Dr Edward, I could not write half the particulars I would
wish to write but I send you a newspaper or two which will
give you more information than I can. With regard to
climate, this country is hot to be sure, but not one-tenth part
as much so as when we arrived in the colony. Now some
may think I say this because we are getting used to the heat
of the climate, but that is not the cause alone. Every year [is]
getting cooler; the opening and cultivating of the land I think
- and I am not alone in my opinion - has a deal to do with it.

The air is dry, open and clear. [There is] no such thing as fever and ague or any of those common maladies that are so prevalent in America, are not so much as known here. The Lord be thanked. To conclude, your aunt with myself send you, your mother and all enquiring friends our most sincere love and respects.

Australia's shape, size and location make it the landmass most completely affected by the great travelling anticyclones, with the resulting heat and dryness, as any global climatic map shows.[8] On to this scenario, Winter tacks his own (and others') interesting version of climatic determinism.

II

Edward Miller did not wait to take Winter's Australian bait because on the 30th day, a Monday at 9 o'clock in the morning, of an unspecified month but probably April 1877, we find him aboard a vessel named the *Douglas* at Liverpool to undertake the long sea voyage to Melbourne, Australia. He wrote home from Liverpool during the preceding weekend.

My ever dear brother, I left Cork at 2 o'clock on Thursday. We spent a fearful night at sea [with] waves mountain high. It blew a fearful gale from 1 to 3 at night. Every passenger a board was sick. We did not get in to Liverpool till 11 at night. At 5 o'clock on Saturday morning the company man came to look for me and took me in charge. I will have to pay 8s-6d. (42¹/₂ p.) for Saturday and Sunday and my breakfast on Monday morning when I board? for Melbourne. I got sea sick about 5 o'clock on Thursday and was bad up to 8 o'clock on Friday morning. I am as right as the mail now, thank God. Now I hope mother and Ann and yourself are all right with God's help. I will write when I land, if with the providence of God, I reach Melbourne. If Peter [9] goes let him stop at 189 Spring Street, Melbourne. Tell Sam Doupe [10] that I hope I will not die till I repay him for his kindness with God's help. The *Douglas* is as fine a boat as I saw in Liverpool. There are not many passengers on board. I do not know a single passenger on board. I was never in better spirits.

With that, the letter ends abruptly; the rest is missing. The voyage out would take in the range of three to four months,[11] which makes 30 April 1877 as the likeliest available date for departing Liverpool.

Later in an undated letter to his mother, Edward reports on an eminently enjoyable voyage out, in contrast to the misery of the short sea crossing from Cork to Liverpool.

> I got very fat while I was on board. We had the best of eating and drinking and very pleasant times. I was a special favourite with all parties on board. I got a drink from the Captain's lady when leaving the ship. I was a special favourite with the Captain. We would [be] together for hours talking on farming. His wife's people were great farmers in Scotland.

Able to ingratiate himself with the Captain and the Captain's lady, Edward appeared set fair to do well in Australia.

III

A letter dated 9 August 1877 finds him having landed in Melbourne and having undertaken a reconnaissance of the city. It also sets the tone for his lengthy descriptive pieces communicated from the antipodes to his old home in Coolybrown.

> Now I have been to all parts in the city and suburbs and every place of note and I must say it is one of the first cities in the world for its age. Any one that saw it in its infancy and see it now, he would rec[k]on it as a first class town. The only thing that I have seen that looked strange in the buildings [is] the little house, then 2 or 3 large blocks as the Yankey term[s] it. But certainly I must say there are as fine a building[s] in Melbourne as are in the world.

Miller again has reason to refer to the incongruity of the Melbourne skyline in a letter of 26 September 1877, while having become more restrained about the merits of its urban landscape (plate 11).

> Melbourne is a fine town but nothing at all near what it is represented to be. George's St. and Patrick St. in Limerick are as fine as you will see in any country you go to. There are some fine buildings in Melbourne and wide streets, but

Plate 11 Melbourne: Tom Roberts' impressionist painting of Bourke
      Street *circa* 1890

one big house and then a little one. It does not look well.
In the larger sense he concedes that nature has been kind to
Australia and in the case of Melbourne's Port Philip Bay 'she has
given it one of the finest bays or harbours in the world.'

Homing in on social conditions in the city, he is soon drawn
into monothematic mood when he fixes upon the demon drink.

> One thing I see in Melbourne is this : I have not seen one
> badly dressed person or one person asking for alms —
> There are in Melbourne poor people. But I have been to
> nearly all places, I might say, and I have seen every
> specimen of poverty, but [the] very little that I have seen is
> certainly from drink. The colonial ail is certainly the curse of
> the colony. I, for my part, I made up my mind with God's
> help never to drink any of it. I tasted it. It does not differ
> much from the English ail. It certainly is the same in colour.
> I always hated ail or perhaps I have been too severe in my
> opinion. But be that as it may, the drinking in Melbourne is
> something fearful. It is nearly impossible to form an
> estimate of what liquor is consumed in Melbourne and its
> suburbs.

Drink and drunkenness count among the major themes in
Australian social history,[12] and Edward Miller's graphic
portrayal of the drinking in Melbourne is the match of anything
to be found in letters home from Australasia.

The same man was soon to be confronted directly with the

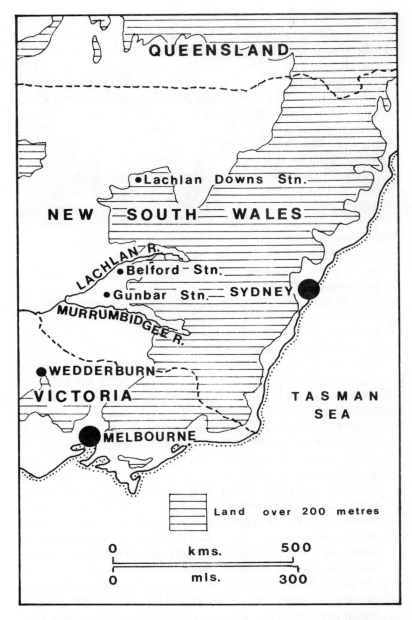

Fig. 11   Edward Miller's sphere in Victoria and New South Wales,
1877-91

effects of drink when he went to Wedderburn to his kinspeople. His letter of 26 September 1877 to his brother Robert contains the following underlined passage.

> I must give you a description of Wedderburn where James Winter and Aunt Tirza [live]. They could be as happy as the days are long but for the curse of the colony, the colonial ail. They both drink very hard. I have been told on good authority that they were worth £1,000 at a time. He treated her very bad and that was the cause she drank. They care for nothing in fact but drink. They have a fine garding [garden?]. It is well kept, but what good is that. As fast as they make a shilling they drink it. He does not give her any money, but she makes out or comes at the blind side of him. But it all goes in drink. They have enough to eat of the best, but that will not do. While I was there I felt wretched and they did not care so far what became of me provided I gave them drink. Let none of the friends see this. I mean in Killeheen or Court.

Such news was meant for purely private consumption and to emphasise the point Miller overwrites the above passage with the instruction: 'Do not read this part of the letter for outside parties that is lined.' He will allow without underlining it that the Winters 'are in good health and could do well now if they gave up drink.'

However, writing to his mother on another occasion, he again goes straight to the nub of the Winters' problem, paying particular attention to his aunt.

> Dear Mother, Aunt is very strong but very much addicted to drink. In fact [she] cares for nothing else, but she has enough as far as the goods of this world are concerned. She recollects scarcely anything about home, but I did not catch her in her right senses yet —- I may not see her now for some time, but she promised me her likeness, and when I get it I will send it home. I need not tell you to say anything about aunt Tirza or James Winter. I believe what is to be will be, but all parties drink hard out here or nearly all. But I have made up my mind with God's help not to drink or gamble or anything foolish. May God in his mercy strenghten me.

Edward Miller proved as good as his word. In a raw and rugged milieu, he was the essence of steadiness and decency.

And he was an excellent observer and commentator on landscape and life, especially when he got out into the backcountry. In his letter dated 9 August 1877, to which it is clear he added incrementally until well into September, he forsakes the city for the country.

There are a few hundred miles of cleared country or plain as the settlers term it about Melbourne. I am now up the country about 150 miles. I have seen where there has been large tak[e]s? of gold and unless where there is a town - and they are very few and far between - you will not see the face of a human being for miles. From what I see of the colony, unless the little cleared about Melbourne, it is certainly a forest life. I saw some of the snakes in a loipside? state. I saw their heads chopped off with the axe. The country people seems very content and happy. The houses are far between, that is if you can call them houses —

I have now seen a great deal of this country. It is rightly named the bush or wilderness, for unless a little patch here and there that is cleared by real black labour and then to settle down and try to make a living where you will scarcely see the face of a human being unless you have a wife for weeks. Why to think of going to a place of worship that is never thought of and yet the people seem contented. Tis a lonely life and not a doubt about [it]. If one could look about them and see the country it would not be so bad, but not the slightest chance of that. [There is] nothing but trees and scrub in every direction. 3 or 4 hundred yds. is the most you could see. To hear parties talking of a plain and call it a big one, 5 or 6 hundred acres would be thought a great sight. But [from] what I saw, it is very flat [and] not much hills. The earth is generally speaking led or brown. I have seen large fields where the gold was got and in great gullies as the diggers call it. But when the gold was plenty and land easy got they, that is parties, who got the gold did not keep it [but] drank and gambled it as fast as they got it. The fact was this, that they thought the gold would hold always.

Miller captures here the speed of the sound of loneliness in little settled country. He paints in an almost primeval landscape and the ambience of 'forest life,' and he touches upon the transience of gold in the mind, the pocket, and the despoliated settings from which it was extracted.

Commenting specifically on the nature of settlement and house types, Miller catches well this raw world in transition and he writes for the most part approvingly about it and about its people, while remembering how things were done at home.

> The houses are very neat inside, but very cool and clean. They are made of laid logs on each other [and] mud laid between the logs. They are covered with bark. Most of them are carpeted, that is the floors with bags, the same as you use with at home to keep wheat. In some of the houses are mere framework and the board[s] are laid on just the same as I laid them on the dairy. [There is] no chance of fill beaming, but the more holes the better. Why in fact the outside of the houses are far wo[r]se than any shed you could see, but the inside makes up for all that! Some have their house covered with galvanise iron. Tis very like zink, but the best of them is nothing that you would call a house, but a mere hut.

The contrast between inside and outside was stark and as items in the landscape, what passed for houses stood in marked contrast to the kind of vernacular architecture that Edward Miller had known intimately in Ireland. Still he tunes in with remarkable facility to an appreciation of Australian homeplaces. He ties people to places.

> Another word for the houses. I certainly say the log hut is the most comfortable. It does not draw half so much air as the frame building, but for all that it has air enough. The house made of framework is too much vintilated, but the summer is something warm. The houses in towns as far as I have seen are covered with galvinised iron or bark. The bark is the best but tis not so stylish. But the people are very neat and stylish and unscrupulously clean. You could not see anything on anyone come out of such houses, I mean as regards the style, the wealth and the comfort of the people.

To finish the passage, he writes: 'You must know that I am a new chum in Victoria yet.' In tuning in to the scene and in describing it, he can only be accounted as doing well for what passed in the Australian idiom as a newcomer.

And he travelled extensively during his first weeks in Australia. In his letter of 9 August 1877, to which he added piecemeal over time, he recounts travelling through Victoria from Melbourne to Seven Hills and through 500 miles of New

South Wales, both on the Murrumbidgee River and the Laghlan (fig. 11). He liked much of what he saw.

> Speak of Australia as an uncivilized country, why in fact I never met nicer people, nor heard the English language, that is to say by all parties, so well spoken, no brogue at all. The only thing that comes strange to me is that every one - no matter [how] poor or rich, big or little, must carry their swag or bed. It consists of a pair of blankets and a billy can, about the size of a two quart saucepan with a handle across and a cover on it. It is used for boiling water to make tea. You can travell over the whole country. It will be no expense. You can stop at every station or house. They all keep travelling. Tis the custom of the country. They will give you going away tea and bread and meat, and when it is dinner times [you] strike a light, make a fire — if you do not see a house or if too lazy to go out of your way.

Ned Miller captures well the egalitarian nature of Australian society, its mobility and its hospitality, while his depiction of a pluralist immigrant community is utterly at odds with the picture presented by his cousin, Ann Miller, when writing home from Buffalo in 1872.[13]

The one thing that he clearly does not care for at all is the dissoluteness induced by gold and by drink.

> Short as I have been in the country, [I] have met hundreds that got thousands of pounds in gold working for their daily wages [and] drank and spent it in fast living. Tis something awful, what vice and misfortune that some men and women fall into. Talk of religion to them, why you may as well whistle a jig to a mile stone![14]

Ned shows his taste for proverbs in illuminating his literary style and his utter distaste for intoxicating liquor. As he puts it succinctly in an Australian context, 'the great evil is drink.'

Having travelled widely but not having earned a shilling from 26 April[15] until 7 September 1877, Ned Miller states with urgency ' I must get work now at any price.' He soon landed a job because on 26 September he was able to report positively to his brother Robert. For an address he used 'the bush, for tis a real life forest.'

> This is a very fine country. The wages are very good. I have £1-5s. (£1.25) — and as for diet it cannot be beat. *Breakfast* as soon as you turn out of bed before you go to work - bread,

meat, that is beef, mutton or bacon, butter, cheese and tea.
Dinner two or three kinds of meat, pudding and tea. *Supper*
the same. In fact tis meat at every meal and besides this
there is lunch twice. You go to work at 7 o'c. You will have
your breakfast, then at 9 o'c lunch, dinner at 12 and an hour
and $1/_2$ for dinner, lunch at $1/_2$ past 3 o'c and supper at   6
o'c. Then the day's work is done. The weather is very fine,
but not over hot yet. Parties tell me it will be fearful hot in
the summer. January and February are the two hottest
months in the summer. —
Nothing in this country for 6 days of the week but work. As
soon as I can I will get a horse and wagon and try another
game. It is not the man that works the hardest that makes
the most money. Tis strange what a little hold parties have
of money in this country. If parties lived in this country as
they do at home a horse would not be able to draw their
money. In fact the diet or eating is beyond description. To
see the sheep of this colony, to look at them you would not
give them grass like a little dog. The parties that sell fat ones
only get 8 or 9 shillings a piece for them. The average price
of meat is $2^1/_2$ pence mutton, beef $3^1/_2$ to 4 pence, pork 4 to 5
pence a lb. Pork is the most prized.

Although he fails to be explicit, we can fit Edward Miller into
the favoured pastoral world of Australia at a time of great
forward changes,[16] and as the materialistic thrust of his evidence
suggests, he fitted admirably into this world.

However, it was by no means all travel first and then work for
Ned Miller. He also partook in possum shooting nearly every
day since he came out, while he was drawn in too to one of the
favourite sports in the colony, i.e. kangaroo hunting.[17]
Describing the latter activity, he reports as follows:

They run on their hind legs. The dogs that hunt them are
very like a greyhound. If the dog or dogs that hunt them
come up the kangaroos will take one of them on his two fore
legs and run to a hole of water and unless the dog is very
strong he will crown? him. They never bite but kick or rip
open with their hind leg. They have one big nail on their
hind legs. If they get a chance, they will rip you open. They
will cut you like a knife, especially if it is an old man
kangaroo. I was at the death of 4 snakes. They are very
plenty[ful and] a beautiful colour.

As with most other facets of landscape and life, Ned Miller was from an early date drawn into familiarisation with the fauna of the backcountry which included possums, kangaroos and snakes, and in the manner of the time he participated in their killing.

Having commented extensively on his new found situation in his letter of 26 September 1877, Ned Miller promises further amplification: ' I will send home my log when I look over it. It will make you all laugh.' He then turns to home thoughts from the antipodes.

> Let me know how all things are going on. How the crops are! Did the wheat do well? How the cows are doing! —— Let me know did B. Lynch go to America or did I. Connell marry her! —— Tell S. Doupe he will have a long letter from me in a few days. Let me know all particulars about that worthy family or as I call them our own now - the Millers of Ballycahane. Peter by this must be married. Let him not think of coming to Australia for to get a wife or if he do he will find his mistakes. [There is] no fortune to be got over here, but to give a fortune to get one.

He conveys his best love to enquiring friends and especially his cousins in Courtmatrix, Killeheen and Ballycahane, and he asks that the reply be directed to him c/o John Winter at Wedderburn, 'be sure not to James Winter!'

We may further amplify upon Ned Miller's early Australian experience in a letter to his mother. This is undated but clearly in the first months after arrival. In it the nature of his work is divulged and also how he favoured staying with John Winter in Wedderburn rather than with John's brother James and Aunt Thirza.

> My Dear Mother, Do not be uneasy about me. I am as well as you can wish me to be and if the Lord leave[s] me my health I will be well off in a little time. I believe the Lord has his wise ends for everything. Glory be to God for his kind mercies to us all. I have £1-5s. a week. The work is pret[t]y hard, pick and shovel, tank making. I like the country well. I am up 300 miles from Melbourne. I staid with John Winter for a good bit. His wife is Cunningham from above Newcastle. She is a near relative to the Mangans in Reens and no mother could do more for me. She was a Roman Catholic, but parties out here make no distinctions like old

> Bigoted Ireland. —— Tell Jim Bennett I wish to God he was
> here. Then he would know the difference —— Tell him that I
> will look sha[r]p to see what this country is and I will let
> him know all particulars.

He promises to soon send his ailing mother a remittance as he is
'in a fair way for it,' and re-echoing the sentiments expressed by
many emigrants to North America,[18] he states boldly and
unequivocally that 'what has Ireland ruined is pride.' With his
own encouragement of Jim Bennett and others, Edward was
doing his bit to add to the trail of long-distance migration out of
a pride begotten and socially segmented homeland.

IV

Having commenced writing home with frequency, Ned Miller
also maintained a long running correspondence with his cousin,
Peter Miller of Ballycahane, and depending upon his
correspondent, it is interesting to note the change in mood, tone
and content of Ned's letters. With Peter Miller, it was a matter
of renewing an old friendship, beginning with the use of a new
idiom. Ned's letter is dated 16 January 1878 and it carries a dual
address. On the one hand, there is the Gunbar Station,
Whealbah, Lachlan River via Hay NSW; on the other, there is
'the bush, for such is my life at present.'

> My old chum, It is with great pleasure in this new country to
> me that I for the first time communicate. Still hoping it will
> find you and all the family in good health as this leaves me
> at present, thanks to Providence. Peter, tis very fine to talk
> of Australia and its gold fields and the great wealth that is to
> be got. I need not tell you that Kerry cows wear long horns.
> My wages at the present are £5 a month. The weather at
> present is very hot and the work very hard. If a fellow was
> heaving water over you, you could not be wetter with sweat.
> The more you sweat, the better you can stand the heat.

Here the writer skilfully exploits a proverb as put-down, while
emphasising the arduousness of the work and the heat of the
sun in the situation in which he finds himself.

He then goes on to fashion a picture of life in the bush which
is stark, comparative and compelling.

Peter, let me tell you parties do not know at home how they are r[e]ared or how other parties live. Tis very fine to say to write home continually. You have not the slightest idea what a bush life is. You will not see the face of a Christian for months and not a post office within 100 miles. No one knows what difficulties one goes through, unless parties that travel. Tis all right with parties that go to a foreign country and settle down in the town. They land in for little or nothing. But start for the backwoods and take your stand there shut out from all society and the buzz and bustle of the busy street? and let me see how they will stand it.

There was, however, something distinctively Australian about this milieu, described with such realism by Ned Miller, which allies pastoral occupance with outback mythology, and which remains to-day as one of the great bulwarks of Australian identity.[19]

None of this impinged upon Miller from Coolybrown. He had his own limited agenda.

I for one came out to Australia for to make money with God's help and it will go very hard with me if I do not fulfil my object. Let me tell you that when I started to work I had only 4 pence, but now I have pounds, thank God. One thing in a bush life is this: all the money goes into the pocket and if you work hard you are very well fed. It is not the work altogether but the great heat and hot winds that will weaken a fellow. But let me tell you, old chum, that on no account be led on by me. For with God's help I will never settle down to make Australia my home. I do not like the country. And while I can make money, as soon as I get what will give me a start at home, I will be back again. I hope with God's help to clear 50 or 60 pound at the least a year.

This is a clear re-statement of Ned Miller's ambitions. He plays down the appeal of Australia, even to the extent of allowing for the first time that he does not like it.

Everything was tempered by experience and by the particular pitch of his letter to Peter Miller.

I have seen a great deal of the country and as for the gold fields, they are played out. Money made now in Australia is by hard work and if a man worked so hard at home he would be as well off [as] stretch under a bit of canvas all the year round, lying on some old bags for his bed. —

Talk of fine clothes, tis all thrash. If you could wear leather,
that is what would suit. You must wash, patch and mend
and do not be surprised to hump your swag 100 or 200
[miles] from one job to another. I can tell you I was one of
the lucky ones from the time that I started up to this. I have
put up something and I hope to continue so. As for women,
it is one of the most wretched shops in creation as far as I
can learn.

He asks in return from Peter ' a good bagfull' of news, before
concluding with an insight into his own highly mobile lifestyle:
'I hardly know where to tell you to direct your letter, for I am
knocking so much about New S. Wales. Chance it thus: Mr.
John Winter, Wedderburn, Victoria, Australia.' With that, he
ends the only extant letter to his ' old chum.'

V

We next encounter Ned Miller in an utterly pastoral setting.
This was on 5 May 1878 when he wrote home to his brother
Robert from the 'North Prary' NSW, having crossed off as an
address the Gunbar Station, Whealbah, Lachlan River via Hay,
NSW. It transpires that he had left his job at tank making[20] on
17 March and was out of work for ten days. Let Ned himself
pick up the narrative!

I took a job of droving on 28 March. I picked up a good
sheep dog and travelled 240 [miles] north. I am now -?
miles north of this prary shepherding 2230 sheep, the one-
third of the flock we brought to the station. Mr. Broomfield
is the owner of the station on which I am shepherd. I have
my horse to ride if I like, or walk. My dog does the work. I
am lying down half the day or more, keeping on reading.
£52 is the wages per year and found. I have to cook for
myself. When I want meat, [I] kill a sheep. I must bake my
own bread. In fact you get flour, tea, sugar and cook for
yourself. I think with God's help I am done with hard work.
Mr. Broomfield is a fine fellow, no pride about him. I like
shepherding. It is a lonely life, but a very quiet one. You are
your own master and you will wear your cloth[e]s unless
setting down. Do not write until I write again. I expect to
be a long time with Broomfield. I earned £6-5s for the five

weeks I was droving. I had to work Easter Sunday as well as any other day. Mind what I tell you. Mind what you have. I might after a little [while] be of some help to you. I will not forget you by any means. I enclose a few sheets giving a right and true account of Australia, as far as I have seen. Preserve these, as I will continue to take notes and send them to you, as I hope with God's help to see you again after some time.

Unfortunately, neither the log mentioned earlier nor these notes survived. However, from what is extant of Edward Miller's correspondence we can adjudge him to be a keen and perceptive commentator on Australian life as he experienced it over the best part of two decades of rapid change.

Reverting to the start of this letter of 5 May 1878, Ned deems himself to have left the low wages of Victoria behind, with his departure to the backcountry of New South Wales. Having forsaken tank sinking for shepherding, he was in his own words ' at the best game in the colony for making money.' Still, life was tough and lonely, as he reminds his brother Robert.

It is nothing to change 2 or 3 shirts in the day. In fact, if you did not sweat well you should look out quick for sunstroke. You said that I knew how you understood why in fact a man has no business of a wife in this country, unless he has plenty of money. Your swag is too much to carry. Mind what you have at home. You have a loving wife, a bed to lie on, and enough to eat.

For once, there is a concession to happy matrimonial circumstance and frugal comforts at home. Australia, as Ned experienced it, was for the single man.

Tell Jim Bennett as a single man he would do well, but with a family he had no business here, unless he had some fast friends. Everything is so uncertain, here to-day and away to-morrow. Then, how could children go along and perhaps no water within 15 or 20 miles, and you must carry rations and bedding along with you.

The peripatetic lifestyle of rural Australia was in Ned's view simply out of keeping with the stability required by the family unit.

And he goes on to amplify, drawing upon his own reservoir of experience.

Let me tell you that I never slept on anything like a bed

since I left home, but after a fellow has a good time at sea he is not particular. The beds that are used are 4 forks driven down in the ground, 2 straight sticks and two shoved up on them. That is the bed. I kept all my bedclothes when I came of[f] the ship and I have them with me in the bush, unless the matrass and my cloth coat that I left at John Winter's in Victoria, where I think they will be safe. I am now more than 400 miles away from his place. He sent your letter to me all right. I had a letter from Sam Winter too and 2 newspapers. I do not intend to make this country my home, only my mind changes. I mean to work steady, keep my money together, that is if it is God's will that I get any health. You might think it strange when I tell you that my funds were all but out when I went to work. But now, thank God, I am worth some -? I am not nearer to a town than 40 or 50 miles —

If Peter Miller comes out to this colony, it will open his eye for him. The climate is very healthy. You can lie down under a tree, roll your blankets about you and sleep sound. But then you have snakes, adders and any amount of insects to look out for, the greater part of which are poisonous. If a bulldog ant get[s] hold of you, he will make [you] jump. The pain is something awful. It will last for hours. Why in fact, parties here are like snails carrying their houses on their backs! Since 11th of October 1877 I never slept in a house, but in calico tents. Now that I am making money fast, I can put up with anything. [There is] no place of worship to go here to, but for all that I am contented. I read a chapter in my bible and give myself up to God.

The atavistic traits of his people - steadiness, godliness, decency and discipline - stood Ned Miller in good stead in the raw world of backcountry Australia, where the people like the snails carried their houses on their backs.

To sustain him, he did the rounds of the family in his early letters home. Another such letter, undated and unaddressed, is directed to his sister-in-law, Anne. The context remains the same: Ned was still the shepherd of sheep in remote country.

My ever dear sister, I know you would be glad that I am doing first rate, my work scarcely exercise and the best of eating and drinking. But I must drink my tea without milk. Now that I am used to it, it makes no difference. There are

no cows on the station, but will be soon. As for the
delicasies of life, I might say I have them if I like. But I must
cook for myself. All the cooks out here are men. I might say
women seldom cook. I will take you some choice skins
when I do go home, but I do not intend to go home for some
time, if the Lord spares me. But man propose[s] and God
disposes.

As a man in a world shaped by masculinity, Ned was well able
to look after himself, while as letter writer his felicitous turn of
phrase and his penchant for proverbs often breaks through.

And he showed sensitive touches by enclosing a feather for
baby Barbara's hat and the promise of help for her mother.

Dear Anne, do not want for a pound or a shilling while I
have it. I told your mother that it would go hard with me if
I would not make you comfortable in Coolybrown. It will
go hard with my word, as I do not intend to marry while in
Australia. My wages are £52 a year and the best of board. It
cost[s] me about £6 a year for boot[s] and clothes. My dress
for 8 months [is] white tites, leggings, a tite white jacket and
a broad leaved hat, light boots and spurs. No coats wore
unless for 2 or 3 months in winter. My dress is like a cricket
dress. [It] must be tight for having all saddle work.

Ned Miller from Coolybrown seems the picture of sartorial
elegance, ranging on horseback over sheep country in New
South Wales.

VI

The next of Edward's extant letters finds him settled with Mr.
Broomfield, in whose employment he means to remain for as
long as he can. This was on 6 March 1879 when he was
corresponding from the Belford Station via Hillston, Lachlan
River, NSW. On the one hand he admits the veracity of the old
proverb, 'a rolling stone gathers no moss': on the other he avers,
'likewise it is high time to gather some sense.'

I am settled for this year 1879. I have a fine place. I never
thought I would be so well off. My young boss made me a
present of a very nice pocket bible and [had] to send to
Sydney for it. You know I was fond of a ride after the
hounds at home. Note that I have any amount of riding and

driving and it agrees with me. Before I got your letter I was
to go with my boss to Hay to bring more sheep, but he
changed his mind and I did not go. I told him to send you a
draft for £11 sterling, which he did in two post office orders,
one for £10 and one for £1. So you see, it is not at all times
that I could send you money. From Belford to Hay is 300
miles. You have no idea what this backcountry is like; I
could not get an order nearer. Let mother want for nothing
while I have a pound. I will not forget her, nor you. Dear
brother, you and I had a long tug? together and I felt it
very much when parting. I did not see what good I could be
to you if I staid with you, but here I can do something for
you and myself. But Providence ordereth all things.

Here is a graphic illustration of backcountry isolation and the
will to breach it by a generous benefactor. Fond remembrances
triumphed over past differences.

Turning to something completely different, Ned Miller
introduces a note of topicality by reporting on the rampaging
Kelly gang and how they fired the popular imagination in
Victoria and New South Wales. The saga of Ned Kelly and his
gang had erupted into open violence, robbery and death in
1878.[21] News and legend alike were disseminated like wildfire.

Victoria and New South Wales are greatly excited by a gang
of bushrangers. They are called the Kelly gang, Ned Kelly
captain. They stuck up two banks, one in Victoria and one
in New South Wales. Both colonies have offered £8,000
reward for their capture. The money taken out of the banks
amount[ed] to over £4,000. The gang consists of 4 men, 2
Kellys and 2 others.

The saga closed as fact but was only enhanced as legend with
the hanging of Ned Kelly for wilful murder on 11 November
1880. 'Such is life,' he is reputed to have said, with the noose
around his neck and the aphorism 'game as Ned Kelly' became
forevermore embedded in the Australian folk tradition.[22]

Apart from this one topical digression, Ned Miller stays with
the mundane concerns of contact with the world and with
family, friends and relations.

You said you would send me a paper a week. You cannot.
There is one mail only, once a month from London. You can
send a paper once every two months and that will do. I can
have any amount of papers but I have only the one of this or

I would send you some. James Delmege [23] and Switzer, I think, could not do better if they keep from drink, but they are gone to a hot shop. This summer was cool [compared] to last summer, 113 [degrees] the highest in the shade and that only for three days. Tell Peter Miller to get married and not to wait till he is too old, or if he is to wait much longer I will be home in time for the wedding, if the Lord spares me. Ten years from this date you can look out for me to visit my native county and settle down. I will not go in double harness while in Australia —

I had an account of Aunt Tirza and James Winter not long since. They are well but I am over 400 miles away from them. One thing I must say: better to be along with strangers than your own. I must say so. For what I got I had to earn it. But thank God I had great luck to face in with the men I did. I am as comfortable as I can wish to be, and good wages, and no fear of getting a blow from the shovel or pick. There are a great many now idle, but it is their own fault.

He resolves to stay put in the employment of Mr. Broomfield and he asks that his address be given to no one. Last words to brother Robert are, as ever, reassuring: 'Do not want for a pound while I have one.'

Stay put he did, because in his next communication of 6 May 1880 we find him still happily in the same employment.

I am with Mr. Broomfield still and likely to continue. He is a perfect gentleman and not a bit of pride about him. I am doing well. My wages are £52 per annum and I clear as much more. I deal pretty heavy in horses, in fact anything I can make a note in. About 2 or 3 hours of a ride does my work every day. [It is] scarcely exercise, but when we are mustering we are in the saddle from dark to dark. My life is a quiet one, properly a bush life, as since I came into N.S. Wales I have never been in town. The nearest town is 55 miles and it is a drunken hole. I do not care to go there. In fact I want to make money and not to spend it, as I hope to be my own master some day. This is a fine climate, as healthy I think as there is in the world. You might not believe me when I tell you that parties sleep in the open air throughout the year. But this year it is very disagreeable, as the winter is wet. May, June and July are winter months.

November, December and January are the summer months.
The notes sounded are all of a kind that may readily be
associated with Edward Miller in his backcountry situation -
discipline, diligence, enterprise, contentment.

On this occasion he was writing to the mother of his 'old
chum,' Peter Miller of Ballycahane, about a matter of great
sensitivity. Relating as it did to inheritance in the context of the
Irish family farm,[24] there could scarcely be a more contentious
issue to be given an airing abroad.

> Dear Mrs. Miller, It is with pleasure that I pen these few
> lines. Still hoping that they will reach you and all your
> family in good health — I had a letter from Peter a few days
> ago and I was horrified to learn that there was not
> unanimity amongst you. He told me you gave him some of
> the land, but no stock nor a house. By what I can learn
> things are looking seedy in Ireland, but I know you could do
> more. Land is no good without stock or capital. I know
> likewise that you have the children to do for. But you know
> Peter is your first born and the sweets of your honey moone.
> And if not your first born, he certainly is his representative
> and I think he should have a very great claim. But if I have
> [in] any way interfered with your feelings I beg a thousand
> pardons. Let me ask you, will barren land yield of itself or
> will you gather figs of[f] thistles? Try Peter with a little
> cultivation. Dig around him as you would a tree and
> manure him with a reasonable start, at the same time asking
> for divine aid. For without it we are as a tickling brass on a
> sounding symbol and I am sure he will not be unreasonable.
> You know where there is union there is strength, better than
> I can tell you.

Coming down strongly on the side of his old chum, Edward
makes a powerful plea for primogeniture, while putting his case
sensitively with metaphorical echoes from the Bible.

And he brings his own weight of moral authority to bear.

> I, though in the far off lands of Australia could not forget
> home nor my brother, though you know when I left home
> he had ten times my means to live upon. But that is not the
> point. It is love we want, that brotherly affection [reflecting]
> the happiest times of our lives when we knew nothing of
> this world's cares in our childhood, and as we grow up and
> mingle with the troubles of the world, I say our bond of

union should grow stronger and stronger, until it is past
bending. Do you think I would let my brother starve when I
could relieve him? No, I never will. Whilst I have a shilling,
he shall have half of it. But I am not laying myself down as
a model. I am speaking my mind. May God direct us all for
the best.

To end, he wishes that his warmest regards be conveyed to his
cousin Julia, and he asks by way of reply that a certain
Neazor's[25] address in New Zealand be sent to him. From his
relative isolation in backcountry Australia, Edward Miller was
actively fashioning, through correspondence, a domain of
impressive proportions.

The great bulk of his correspondence, however, went home
and on 8 November 1881 he writes again to Coolybrown, to
Robert and Anne.

Thank goodness, shearing is over and I might say hard work
is over for the next twelve months (plate 12). For the last six
weeks I had some fearful saddle work. I had five men with
me most of the time. But I had all the responsibility and I
am glad to say Mr. Broomfield has a very good return, for he
is worthy of it. He has 50 tons of wool — A great many
squatters are very badly off for grass and water and if there
is not rain soon, [there will] be great losses in stock. It is a
very dry season throughout Australia in general and in
some of the agricultural districts the crops are all dead for
want of rain.

Drought counts persistently among the major types of
catastrophic event to affect farming in Australia. Beginning in
1880, it caused the cropped area to contract, while in the 1890s it
set limits to the expansion of the pastoral industry.[26]

Turning to the content of Robert's last letter to him, Edward
makes it clear that the married brother at home was adept at
taking a rise out of his bachelor brothers abroad.

You mentioned a young lady in your letter and you tells me
to mind number one. I cannot make it out. Let me know
what you mean. Do not speak in riddles. I made a fool of
myself once and it is not likely I will do so again with God's
help. But what would or will you say when I tell you that a
very nice young lady sent me some of what God gave her
and let me tell you that I will do my best to keep it. So you
see, though far away that I am, I am not forgotten. But my

> dear brother and sister, I will not do anything that will cause
> you any uneasiness while the Lord spares me in Australia. It
> is my full intention to go home after some time if I am
> spared. [Whether] I will stop at home or not is another
> thing. I see that Ireland is very much disturbed at the
> present time and I see that there is great reduction in the
> rents. But I think still that there are other reasons for
> complaint.

Edward kept in close touch with the so-called Land War in
Ireland and the implications of the Land Act of 1881 were well
known to him. He was an avid reader of both Irish and
Australian newspapers and a keen writer and receiver of letters.

Furthermore he offers ample proof, even within the confines
of this single letter.

> I should have answered your letter of 12 July long ago, but I
> sent you a paper off and on and will send you any that are
> worth sending, but there is very little news in them. Now I
> am glad you are doing business for Mrs. Gibbins.[27] It will
> pay you. I do not see why you could not spare a day in the
> week. I only got one of the papers, the *Freeman* —
> I had a letter from Wm. Wills - a very good one, and I think,
> a letter from Peter Miller by its stile, but there was no name
> to it. They came by the same mail. I did not hear from
> Jimmie Delmege for some time. When last I heard, he was
> well. Ask John Switzer in Court how his son likes
> Queensland?[28] Send me his address and I will write to him.

Staying assiduously in touch, Edward was always at the ready
to extend his range of contacts.

And keeping up the correspondence with home, there is
another letter to Robert and Anne on 4 September 1882, again
from the Belford Station. At home the Land Act of 1881 was
apparently about to be transmitted into lower rents, while away
in Australia, Ned Miller professed himself well satisfied with
life.

> I am glad you have such good prospects of coming to a
> proper understanding with your landlord and that your
> hopes will be realised. I sincerely wish it. I have first rate
> times at present. I am in charge of 40 horses about 8 miles
> away from the station on grass.[29] It is open country for
> hundreds of miles. Still I might say I have scarce nothing to
> do. Everything in this backcountry was up to famine prices.

[In] some places flour [was] one shilling per lb. and other
things according[ly]. Carriage was so high - 25 shillings for
oats per bushel of 40 lbs. and hay from £50 to £60 per ton.
So you can judge how the state of the country was. But this
season is opening better. There is plenty of grass now for
stock, but nothing for horses and I think I will be out of the
mustering for shearing which I am not sorry for from this
forward. I will save all my money and I intend to have a
look at you all if I am spared for some time, though I have
now what is not to be snift at.

Climatic conditions once again intruded. When benign,
everything with the world was good. When malign on the other
hand, things were wretched. Commenting on the previous
summer, Ned Miller deemed it 'a terror, so dry and hot, enough
to turn any one gray, no matter whether young or old. In fact
ma[n]y parties are ruined here on account of the loss they
sustained in stock.' In the Australian outback, seasonal moods
and psychological moods were intertwined.

To relieve monotony and to stay in touch with home and with
the world, Ned Miller kept up a broad range of contact.

I have written to Mrs Magner[30] and given her all the
information I could. If she wants more she can write to me.
I send you a paper with this. If you [send] a paper let [it] be
the *Examiner* or the *Chronicle*. I do not care about the
Freeman. I knew Jimmy Delmege was at Nlannifer? I had a
letter from him there, but it was more than 18 months [ago].
So I thought he left it. I wrote to Uncle Jacob letting him
know that James Winter was dead.[31] I wrote to Uncle Jacob
before and never got an answer. I also wrote to Mary
Anne[32] and never received a reply. So if I do not get a reply
I will write no more. Say nothing about it.

Here at the end is evidence that while the Irish kinship
mentality travelled well and travelled far, it could gradually
crumble due to lack of reciprocity in sending and receiving.[33]

From the Belford Station, Edward Miller again writes home -
on this occasion separately to Robert and Anne - on the 25th of
an undisclosed month in 1883. To Robert, he reports on the two
types of natural catastrophe to visit the pastoralist in his
backcountry setting or the agriculturalist in his district of high
tillage.

This season up to now has been dreadful but now that the

drought is fairly broke up things will look better. It is awful
to see stock in thousands perish for want of water and grass.
In some of the districts in this backcountry sheep and cattle
farmers has had very severe times of it and in some of the
agricultural districts the crops are all gone back into the
ground. In fact the last three years I might say was one
continuing drought. But this season now just on is opening
up very cheerful [with] very heavy floods on before. One of
the creeks or as you would call it a river rose up over 7 or 8
feet in less than an hour and about 400 yards wide, a regular
wall of water taking everything before it when it came here.
I have seen hailstones as large as pullets eggs, but I never
said so, though there are very heavy falls on the mountains.
This summer will be good, I think, owing to the large
quantity of water, though God knows the last three has been
hot enough.

If the Canadian West lies poised on a knife edge between the
terrors of frost and drought, then equally the pastoralists of
backcountry Australia have had to contend with the extremes of
flood and drought,[34] as Ned Miller makes clear in the 1880s.

Following on from this, it is worth noting the writer's
contrasting evaluations of life in exile, depending upon whether
he is addressing his brother Robert or his sister-in-law Anne.
With Robert, as man to man, brother to brother, everything fares
well with the world.

The climate agrees first class with me. I have good health
since I came to the colonies, thanks to Providence. I think
this is one of the healthiest climates in the world. You can
see parties sleeping in the open air the whole year round.

With Anne on the other hand, the focus is softer and the tone
more free and more frank.

My dear sister, I hope if I am spared to see you again as I do
not think I will ever settle down in Australia. I do not like
the country some how. When I think I have competency to
keep me, I shall take a trip home, if I am spared. I hope then
to be of some help to some one.

There is perhaps far less contradiction here than may be
supposed at first glance. Back to back letters to a man and a
woman, a brother and a sister (in-law) simply show up
differently in what may be seen as complementary forms of
epistolary address.

As for the rest, there is accordance when the focus switches back on to the homeland and the world of kinship. In his letter to Robert, Ned makes mention of a recent letter from Peter Miller of Ballycahane with all the news. Peter's sister Sarah was about to marry Robert Delmege,[35] while his sister Emily had become bedridden. As for Peter himself, Ned Miller remains puzzled about his continuing state of bachelorhood. He writes to Anne:

> I cannot make it out how Peter is not married. Surely he is not born odd or turned a woman hater. I copied a piece out of a paper I sent Peter. It is on friendship. I sent Peter the paper, so that he can study it. It is well worth reading —
> He said Bob had a fine son, but I told him it was you that had it.[36] I hope you do not spoil him by too much petting. Peter said he spent a jolly day lately in Coolybrown. He said the Delmeges were there. He said Miss Delmege is a very fine young woman. He said Mary Anne went to America. None of them write to me this long time. Your sister Sarah I think is following suit. She has stopped too. I believe I must have offended some way or another. Still I suppose I must paddle my own canoe and I thank my God that has given me the ways. Is Miss Mick married yet? I suppose if she was Peter would tell me, as he gives me all the news.

An old bond of friendship remained firm, while others wilted. The links with home proved steadfast and the incremental news of the neighbourhood reached a native son in a distant part of the world. Dissemination either way came with the mail, and for his part Ned in Australia could be counted upon to send, as well as to receive and facilitate.

The next of his extant pieces, addressed to his sister-in-law Anne, hails yet again from the Belford Station. Only a short note, it is dated 10 June 1885.

> The reason I write is simply this. I had a letter from your sister Sarah [37] about this time twelve months, as near as I can judge. There was no date to her letter. She told me about the young man from Newport and a great deal of news. In fact, it was from her I used to hear all the news. But I suppose she has found a sweet heart this Shrove and so good by[e] to far off Ned in Australia. Be good enough to enquire if she has got an orange silk necktie that I sent her in a newspaper

or if it arrived in Rath[keale].

As to news of his own, he heralds a proposed break from the backcountry.

> I am thinking of having a trip to Victoria as I can get vacation for two months, and if I do not get spliced, I will have you all looked at and then spend the rest of my days in Australia.

Obviously by now well attuned to the Australian vernacular, he had not the least notion of getting married. With one agenda only, he was dogged and sometimes amusing in his pursuit of it.

> You would laugh if you see me riding out with a lady's riding habit on. I am training two of my horses to carry a woman. It is always a pound or two and there's value in good horses.

Always the eager entrepreneur, Ned Miller was determined to make the most in a monetary sense of his Australian experience.

And he took that same spirit with him from the country to the city because on his first break of any consequence we find him reporting on horse racing in Sydney in which two of his own horses participated. This was in a letter to Robert dated 8 April 1886 and addressed from Belford Station.

> I had two horses to race and I waited till the races were over. My mare Modesty has won three races and last Saturday she had a walk over. All the others scratched. The horse, though a nice looking beast and well made cannot stay. He ran third. He is very fast for a short distance. Mind, the mare ran against the horse. I had the two in the race, one to do the running for the other. Nine started. The mare won as she liked. She is $15^1/_2$ hand[s] high. If she goes on all right, she will be worth something handsome when she is five year old.

In both rural and urban situations while in Australia, Ned Miller from Coolybrown could be relied upon to turn his love of horses to good account.

His urban stopovers, however, were short and contrary to expectations of a long holiday in Sydney he could only afford eight days as his boss, Mr. Broomfield, took ill. It proved more than enough for Ned who by this stage was inured to backcountry living.

> I was full up of Sydney. It is a very crowded town [with] very narrow streets and narrow frontage to the houses. I

like the suburbs and the scenery is magnificent and [there is] a splendid harbour. But the business portion of the town is too crowded — I like the people of Sydney first rate. [They are] very homely and nothing stuck up about them and the living there is very cheap. But employment is very scarce and even at reduced wages cannot be got. In fact there is but very little doing in the country. Hundreds [are] looking for employment.

Unlike the vast bulk of rural immigrants issuing into the cities of North America or Australia from post-Famine Ireland,[38] Edward Miller was repulsed by, rather than drawn to, urban life.

And turning to his rural milieu at Belford Station, Ned reports in the usual vein to his farming brother in Ireland.

This summer was not hot, not too much rain at Christmas, but no rain since and the country is looking very parched. If it does not rain it will be a hard winter on stock, though there is good grass on Belford [and] it is not overstocked. There are only four paid hands on the station and no more will be employed till lamb marking. All the improvements are finished or nearly so at least for this year. I do not know about going to see you. Everything seem[s] in so great a ferment. I believe there will be a Civil War yet in Ireland.

Ultimately Ned Miller's last sentiment proved prophetic though not along the cleavage lines that were apparent *circa* 1886.

As for his own going home, he would be accorded a warm welcome to judge from all the tokens he sent.

I hope you got the post office order for two pounds for a dress for Bab. I sent her two silk handkerchiefs for neckties and an orange handkerchief to Peter Miller. It was rather bulky, and do my best I could not fold it tight. Inquire did he get it. In two papers I send with this, you will find a handkerchief in each paper for Bab's two sisters — I expect to be in Melbourne about Christmas when I will send Anne something for old acquaintance.

In return, all Ned wanted was news.

Send me some news when you answer this. Tell F. Adams that I never heard from his sisters? on the woman in Melbourne. Let me know how is Michael McNamara and you can tell him I have got a good racer and that I mean to let him know how she she will turn out on the turf. It costs but very little here to keep a horse.

Adams and McNamara were local blacksmiths and even at a far remove no men could be better placed to appraise the qualities of a racehorse as promising as Ned Miller's mare, Modesty. She was surely the talk of Coolybrown.

VII

Edward Miller's next communication with home finds him having moved decisively northwards to take up a post as stockman on Lachlan Downs Station near Cobar in New South Wales. Here he was in frontier country as the limits of pastoral occupation had only spread there in the decade 1875-85 [39] (fig. 12). The sheep flocks had moved inland into pasture

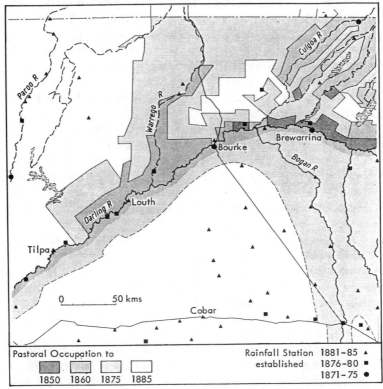

Fig. 12   Pastoral settlement in western New South Wales and the dates of the first rainfall records (after Marshall, 1978)

intermittently grazed by free roaming marsupials. And settlement had moved rapidly into a climate which in its aridity and variability was totally unlike anything encountered before in the British or Irish tradition. As for Ned Miller himself, the recency of his move to Lachlan Downs is apparent in a letter to brother Robert on 8 June 1887.

> My Aunt wants me down to Victoria but I do not care about going down. Besides, I have got a very comfortable situation and I mean to mind it for a little longer. It is very hard to get a good situation now here. There is nothing doing only what must be done. In fact they - that is the land holders - got too great a gruelling those years past. But if the seasons continue like this they will recover quick. If you borrow money the interest is very high. From about the middle of August to the first of November I will be very busy lamb marking and shearing. What made this year so hard was the two lamb markings [and] double mustering.

In a situation of scarcity, Ned's new job was welcome, and all the more so in sheep country where permanent labour requirements were minimal.

He was, however, by this stage beginning to feel the weight of his years in the backcountry.

> I feel rather poorly, but nothing to prevent me from doing my work. I think I have been too much on my feet. I do not care for riding as much as I did, though seldom a day passes but I am in the saddle, little or much, and sometimes for six or seven hours at a stretch, and slow riding. I feel (it) very fatigued. But it is one comfort: I have first class horses to ride.

Now advancing well into his middle years, Ned in his new situation was beginning to feel the pace.

Yet he still kept up the continuum of home thoughts and home contact, and was ever the beneficent brother and uncle. His niece Barbara was a special favourite.

> I will send Bab some skins if I can trap them. They are Bilbies, the best furs in Australia. I have one nearly cured. I will send it in about three weeks or a month. I neglected it a little in the curing. It is so hard to get the oil out of it, but I will be more careful with the next I get. There are two men trapping rabbits and all they chance to get I have arranged with them for the skins. I have got some Emu eggs too. I

> can send them home without going to Sydney. I will send
> you six or eight. There is a parcel post now between Sydney
> and the United Kingdom, but I will have to enquire into its
> workings. It will not cost much: they are only the shells.
> And if I am spared to see you all, I will get them mounted
> and make cups of them. I have two sizes and other things.
> I will save now that I am thinking of seeing you in earnest.
> It will go very sad with me if I will not bring home with me
> some curios.

However, to temper his thoughts of a homecoming he
interposes elsewhere in the letter the remark: 'I see Ireland is
very much disturbed just now and I am afraid it will for some
time to come.'

The rest is taken up with family matters.

> This fine boy of yours that is like me that I hear so much
> about, tell him to be a good boy and I will be a good uncle to
> him yet if I am spared. But Bab is my favourite, though I
> have not seen her — I see by Anne's note some time back
> that she was not very well. I hope she is all right and strong
> again. The blessing of health is one of the very great
> blessings of the Almighty and we do not know the good of it
> till we are deprived of it. But we must be all thankful, for
> we have more than we deserve.

Ned adds as postscript: 'Please remember me to the friends.'

The next letter home follows in the writer's own words 'after a
long silence,' although in fact it came only seven months after
his last known communication. Again directed to Robert, it is
dated 12 January 1888. The perceived delay in writing is
explained straightaway.

> The reason I did not write sooner was I had not made up my
> mind to stop or go home. But as my billet is so good, I will
> stop another season if I am spared. I am pretty well in
> health but I get a pain in my right knee and it last[s] for
> days sometimes. I think sometimes it is gout. But I think it
> is rhumatism, though I have too much exercise for either. I
> feel it very troubles[ome] at times and cannot sleep for
> hours. But I hope it will wear away.

For the first time since he came out, health was becoming a
factor in Ned Miller's enjoyment of life in the setting he mostly
identified with, i.e. the backcountry of New South Wales.

There were other troubles too to add to his personal distress.

Pastoral Australia had its own structure, organisation and dynamic, and above all a kind of stressful seasonality revolving around mustering and shearing, where things could - and frequently did - go wrong.[40]

Plate 12 A typical shearing shed scene exquisitely depicted in Tom Roberts' painting 'the golden fleece'

There was some trouble at shearing - rousabouts striking for more wages and when they were replaced then the shearers struck and went away. So by the delays on both sides shearing went very late. In fact there are a few to be shorn yet. And so by that means all station hands were kept very busy - I mean the permanent hands - and no chance to get away. So Bab will have to wait for the machine for some time yet, as it is only now the sheep are settling for the season and we must see that they go to water, though plenty of rain this season.

Still for all the stress induced by striking seasonal workers, the work, as always, got done, and out from a gathering adversity came a plenteous supply of water for the sheep returning to pasture.

Indeed in an area apt to experience extremes of drought and flood, precipitation, when it came, could come in torrents.

Where I live, there was a hail storm or shower as you would call it. It killed 18 fowles and the noise was like a battery of artillery on the iron roof. I do not want to see such another storm. It was the 29 December in [what] I might [call] mid summer. In one hour 3$^1/_2$ inches of rain fell, so you can judge [for   yourself] — This is mid summer here now. It is called a cool on the glass - only 106 as yet - but it is [getting] very hot here now.

Well aware of rainfall measurement at one of the many local stations around Cobar (see fig. 12), Ned Miller, like most long-distance migrants, was sensitively attuned to the vagaries of climate in a far-off land.

Then to finish, he renews the trunkline of news and enquiry to home.

I had a letter some time back from Peter Miller, but very little news in it. He told me he did not go to law with his father.

If you know what part of Australia Jimmie Delmege is in you might let me know, though do not go to any trouble about it, or if there is any account of Sam Doupe, or how he is doing. Why did Willie Odell go to America? How are the Odells doing? Is there any account of Bob Doupe [41] and how he is weathering it out? Remember me to Mr. Wills and tell him I am thinking of going home in a short time. Give him my best respects. Remember me to the Delmeges and tell Aunt Eliza that Aunt Tirza is now on crutches, but her health is pretty good. Remember me to the Court people, Kiltane and Ballycahane people.

Aunt Thirza was still there to the good in Victoria, having lost her husband of 46 years in 1882. So was her sister-in-law, Eliza Delmege of Killeheen, and the network of kin in old familiar places.

In May of the same year Edward was again in touch from Lachlan Downs, this time enclosing a post office order for £5 to accompany a short note. In it he updates the weather report.

This season has been very dry since the New Year. We had one inch of rain a few days ago which was a great relief to us boundary riders, as the lands got a fair supply of water. — Now we have only to look at the fences about once a month. I expect to be in town about Christmas when I will send Bab a new hat. But the seasons vary so much that you cannot rec[k]on on any time here. I did not write to Jimmy Delmege yet. I had to ride 60 miles to send you this trifle, but if I do not go home I will send you in a short time

something that will give you a start. I see by your letter that
Ireland is far from being settled and until there is some
tranquillity I think I am better as I am.

To finish, he asks that his beloved niece Barbara write to him,
while also looking for a response from his brother Robert.

The next item to be encountered is out of synchronisation with
everything else. Dated 11 June 1888, it issues from a firm of
Sydney estate agents and is directed to Edward Miller,
stockman, Lachlan Downs Station, Cobar. Having duly referred
to signed contracts for six model blocks in what we
subsequently learn is Albany in Western Australia, this
communication shows the man from Coolybrown as property
entrepreneur in Australia. A fresh contract was enclosed for
another detached block which required the purchaser's
signature and return of same. The episode shows how close
Ned Miller's ear was to the ground. It also attests to his enterprise in staking a claim to development land in an incipient
town within a colony about to be thrown open to immigration
(fig. 13).

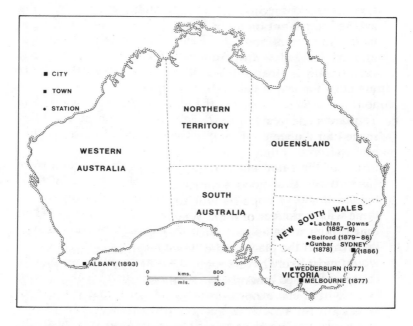

Fig. 13   Edward Miller's Australian world, 1877-93

As well as a new line of investment, the old trunkline to home held firm and Ned's next extant letter comes in answer to one from Robert dated 20 May 1889. Ned's reply from Lachlan Downs is dated 8 July 1889. This suggests for one thing an appreciable improvement in the speed of postal delivery. It also betrays a sense of urgency which reveals itself following hard upon the usual epistolary opening.

> I am glad you have your rent paid. You did not give me all the information I wanted but it does not matter. About the 20th of next month I will send you £10. I could not disturb a fixed deposit or I would lose my interest. I will get my half yearly account from the bank. It will be a bank draft, if I can manage it with the manager. If I have to go to town it will be a post office order. But it will be all the same with you. You will get the £10. It is not much but it may keep you going.

For the brother farming at home there was the promise of £10 to help in lean times; for the brother shepherding away from home there was the resolve to help out, notwithstanding matters of distance and fixed deposits. The bond was past bending.

Next Ned focuses upon the potentially explosive issue of land alienation as exemplified by the Doupe farm in Courtmatrix. Here Harry Doupe's[42] difficulties and departure for Australia had unleashed an instability, still to be resolved. Edward admits surprise, expresses an interest, and counsels extreme caution.

> Your letter seems a great surprise to me about Henry Doupe started for Australia. I shall be glad to see Harry and make him welcome. I think Harry will find Australia a hard road to travel. But nothing venture[d] nothing had. I can set Harry down to as good a dinner as he ever sat down to in his old home. I hope he will keep away from drink and there will be no fear of him. Why did you not let me know that things were as bad with Harry Doupe? Had I but know[n] that the place would be sold eighteen months ago I would most likely have bought some of it at least, but since things are settled amongst the brothers it is as well perhaps. For I would have nothing to do with it, whilst it is so situated. (But now I caution you, if Harry Doupe's place is to be sold, let me have timely notice and it will be hard line[s] if I do not get some of it for you or myself, perhaps all

of it. Mind, keep this secret and no boasting about it! If I see
Harry I will know how things are). Try and find out how
much Harry owes his brother Robert and let me know as
soon as you hear. I think Aunt Eliza might know. You
might ask her on the quiet, but do not let her know on any
account that I bid you. Now I will depend on your
discretion. I will write to Robert Delmege by next mail.
Caution your wife not to say a word about what is in this
letter. Show it to no one!

Advocating here the restrained use of the grapevine accessible
to kin, Edward makes a first, tentative move for the Doupe farm.
His was a keen appraisal of the power of information among
those who possessed it. Equally it was important to define lines
of exclusion, while eyeing the prize.

Family matters *per se* came last.

I am very sorry that my little pet Bab is so delicate. I hope
by the time you get this she will be all right. I am glad the
Delmeges did not sell out and that you and them are on
such good terms. You never seem to say much about your
people in law. I hope ye are not on bad terms.

Not for the first time among the Millers, lacunae in a letter
received abroad had set speculative thoughts in train about the
ins and outs of the family at home.

As for the promise of £10 to help tide Robert over, Ned proved
as good as his word. Indeed the alacrity with which he
responded to a fraternal need is apparent in his letter of 5
August 1889. Enclosed with it was a bank draft for £10. For his
own part, Ned was thriving.

I have done very well this half year, in fact the best since I
have been in the colony, as I nearly cleared two pounds a
week. I did some business for three firms in Sydney and got
five per cent commission.

Even in the frontier country of New South Wales, the man from
Coolybrown was able to uphold a keen sense of entrepren-
eurship, the interests of which ranged across the continent, from
Sydney to Albany.

The domain of kinship was also a vital cog in his cosmos. Ned
reports on the latest of his cousins to hit Australia.

Harry Doupe arrived in Sydney about two weeks ago. I had
a letter from him the second day after he landed and by
what he saw of Sydney he seems to be full of it. He said

business was very dull and he asked my advice about
coming into the country, but you know I never advise. If
Harry comes into the country he will be like a fish out of
water. He will have to carry his bedding and cooking
utensils and have to be his own slusher and washerwoman.
As soon as he get[s] employment, he will find things
different. I hope he will pay me a visit, though I will not
have much time to spare as we will be shearing at the latter
end of the month, and if he comes the way it is most likely
he will get work. I think he feels a bit downhearted, but he
will get over that after he knocks about the country for a few
years. If I was in Harry's place and had - as I dare say he
has - 30 or 40 pounds, I would go straight to Western
Australia. The labour market in NS Wales is overstocked,
but whilst shearing lasts one cannot go wrong for work. But
in a month or two shearing is over.

The choices facing 'new chum' Harry Doupe are set out
cogently, while Ned's own preference for Western Australia
accords perfectly with the venturesome spirit of the Millers,
once new worlds became revealed to them.

As for his own pre-occupations just then, the arduous work of
mustering was bound to prove consuming.

We boundary riders think six weeks a long shearing, for we
have to be in the saddle from dark to dark and a fresh horse
every day. But since the drought broke up, the season is a
very good one and the sheep are in rare buckle? [They] can
go like hares. What one wants are good stopping dogs [43]
and thank goodness I have a splendid pair. I will show
Harry Doupe some nice work if he should come my way.

In sheep country as Ned Miller avers, the link between man,
horse and dog was the sustaining one.

Ranging beyond it, there was the world of kin, the
strengthening bond of Irish-Australian interconnection, and the
promise of a new life chance.

I sent Robert Delmege a note not long since. Tell him when
you see him that I had a letter from Henry Doupe. If my
cousin Miss Delmege [44] is coming out to Australia would
[you] ask her she bring me a few things. Tell her I
will pay her well for her trouble. Enquire of the post master
in Rathkeale if there is a parcel post to NS Wales and if there
is ask him how large a parcel can come. Tell Miss Delmege

> to bring me out a wife or to send me a line. The chances are
> when I leave Lachlan Downs I will either go and see you or
> go to Western Australia and settle there. Even now there is
> a very good opening in Albany, but I want to wait till W.
> Australia has its own government. I think it will be the
> coming colony yet, if once immigration is started. The
> climate of Albany is the best in the world.

With his property investments already in Albany, Western
Australia was there for the taking. But like most things with the
phlegmatic Ned Miller, it could wait.

And wait it did, because Ned's next extant communication
with home again originated in Lachlan Downs on 1 October
1891. On this occasion he penned a short note to his favourite
niece Barbara, who was by then almost fourteen years old.

> I thought before this that I would be in town and send you a
> present. But there are contractors here and, as I have to
> attend to them, I could not get away. [There is] about one
> hundred miles of wire netting[45] to keep out the rabbits
> going on here and some tank sinking. But do not fear, I will
> not forget you — I have plenty to do and long hours in the
> saddle. Some evenings I feel very tired and weary, though
> thank God I have very good health.

Rapidly approaching the age of 55, Ned Miller was by that stage
finding the pace of the range demanding.

His links with kin remained unaffected and he instances
contact from his two most recently arrived cousins in the
antipodes.

> I had a letter from Louisa Delmege a few days ago and one
> from Harry Doupe. They are all well. He told me Mr.
> Preston[46] bought Court and that his brother will keep the
> warren. I do not think that Henry Doupe finds Australia the
> place he thought it was. But Sydney must have some
> attraction for him as I think he has been in Sydney since he
> landed.

Still hugging urban Australia more than two years after arrival,
Harry Doupe's behavioural pattern formed a standing contrast
with that of his cousin from Coolybrown.

VIII

And yet the latter finished his Australian days in an urban

context by going eventually to Albany [47] and writing from there on 6 September 1893. By then Ned Miller had set in motion the steps for an Irish homecoming. According to his note of 6 September, he had that very day posted a registered letter directed to himself at Coolybrown. He asks brother Robert to be very careful of it and not to open it on any account. There was to be only one exception.

> But in case of anything happening to me, I leave you the whole conten[t]s of said letter contain[ing] ten P.O. office orders. Mr. Broomfall? is the post master of Albany, Western Australia.

Then on 9 September there is the all-important addendum.

> I leave in the Orient mail boat bound for Tilbury, London, and will come on as I can arrange, if all goes well. I will see you all by Oct. 20th.

Hope and promise were about to take concrete form.

And to further clarify the details, there was a note in transit, emanating from the Orient Line, RMS "Ormuz," in Naples, on 6 October 1893. It is addressed to Robert Miller.

> All well up to this, thank God. You will get this note three days before I arrive in London. [I] will come on direct, so you can expect me about Monday or Tuesday at Rathkeale railway station, 16 or 17 October. I[f] you are not very busy I would wish you [to] meet me there. Do not open the letter directed to myself, Edward Miller, Coolybrown, Reens, Co. Limerick, Ireland, as it might get you into trouble. But take the greatest care till you give it to me. You will find a letter for yourself with a post office order for £5. I will be able to give you a fair start if all goes well with me when I get home.

With the promise of a start not for himself but for his brother, we come to the end of an Odyssey. The world closes in. With Ned's homecoming there is no more from the pens of the Miller brothers and a remarkably fine exposé on the nature of a family's participation in the great diaspora closes. But for the riches revealed by the correspondence to the old home at Coolybrown and its preservation there, we would at this remove scarcely know anything of the members of an ordinary family who became extraordinary through their global wanderings. They were truly voyagers, with the world as their oyster.

Chapter Six

Transitions : Ireland and the World
1893 - 1956

Mr Robert Miller, hardworking man, ploughing stubbles, 3 days ploughing, harrowing, second ploughing, second harrowing, third ploughing[1]

I am getting good health and that is [the] main thing. There is no chance of me going home — I could not stand the Irish climate now.[2]

I

With the return of Ned Miller to the Miller household at Coolybrown, it is almost as if his life goes into abeyance, because contrary to the impressive written record of his Australian sojourn in the period 1877-93, we are provided with only snippets of him thereafter. The first such snippet entailed the bequeathal of his interest in Albany property blocks to his favourite niece Barbara and to his brother Robert, to be disposed of among the latter's family as he so wished. This was on 19 November 1893, only a month after his arrival home. The text is as follows:

I, Edward Miller, bequeath to my niece Barbara Miller certificate of title, register vol. XXVI fol. 264 for lot 35 Albany model blocks, Western Australia, in the Plantagine location containing 2 acres 3 roods and $6^1/_2$ perches. Bounded on the north by boundary road, east [by] boundary street, west [by] junction street, south [by] block 34 containing 1 acre 2 roods and 8 perches. I, Edward Miller, bequeath to my brother, Robert Miller, a certificate of title registered vol. XXVI fol. 263 for lots 9, 10, 11, 12, 24 and 25 in the same estate, Albany model blocks, Western Australia, containing 4 acres 0 roods $36^1/_2$ perches. Bounded on the north by Costigan Street, on the south by Marbelup Road, on the west by Silver Street, on the east by Cordillera Street,

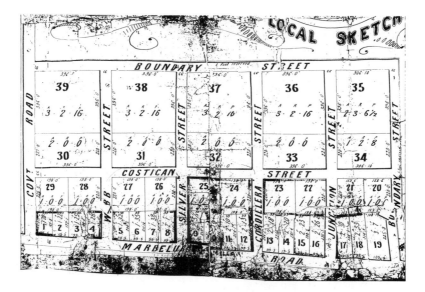

Fig. 14   The Albany property blocks of Edward Miller

to be disposed by him as he thinks just among his children, but Barbara Miller, his eldest daughter, to have no claim or right to any of the said blocks but 35 block, as stated above.

The same model blocks (fig. 14) were subsequently a matter of lively interest and curiosity when devolved upon Rose, the youngest but one of Robert Miller's daughters.

As for her uncle Ned back from Australia amid a bustling household, he quickly settled in to one of his great animations, indeed something which permeates the whole Miller ethos, and that is the abiding love of horses. Ned was the quintessential horseman. As his Australian experience shows, he rode and raced horses and bred and dealt in them. Witness then this little give-away note directed to him at Coolybrown from one Michael O'Leary, of Fourhane, Listowel, Co. Kerry, which is dated 22 May 1895.

I want on receipt of this note to know if your mare proved in foal of my horse. If so, I hope you will be kind enough to let me have a reply by return or meet me in Newcastle West on next Thursday week.

For Ned Miller the love of horses translated with apparent ease into the commitment of a lifetime.

As for his status upon returning we find the record bare, except for his enumeration in the census of 1901 as a farm labourer.[3] He thus returned to the same position from which he had departed all those years ago, except that now he could take on the role of kindly mentor to a growing family, as well as supporting and being sustained in return by their parents. He had, of course, stayed a bachelor and the only discrepancy relates to his age which is given at 55, instead of the 64 years he had then attained. Ned lived out the rest of his life at Coolybrown. He had come back to stay in loving relationship with the intimate surroundings that he knew so well and he died in Coolybrown on 31 May 1907. There is but one little tribute to him which comes from Sarah Miller of Ballycahane and Garrenroe,[4] a sometime correspondent from his own Australian days. Writing to her niece at Coolybrown, she tempers hope with loss.

> I hope your father is strong. He must be very lonesome after
> poor Edward. He was a good brother. He lasted very short.

A good and kindly man had been swept away to eternity, having left his mark indelibly in the annals of Coolybrown.

II

Charged with the support of a young family, Robert Miller also made his mark. This manifested itself best upon the farm at Coolybrown where he continued to be moved by the spirit of improvement. And so we find him through the 1890s and the early 1900s attesting to a whole range of improvements in settings as intimately diverse as fallow garden, hill garden, haggard, hill top, back of barn field and river garden. In January 1896 in the fallow field a fence was being made and quicks being planted; in 1897 there was the making of 50 perches of stone drains and the levelling of 16 perches of fenced quick. Additionally in the hill garden, 80 tons of stones were grubbed and at the top of Coolybrown hill four large boulders comprising 30 tons of stones, were blasted. Ten perches of a car passage was levelled. In October 1901 there was the building of a new horse stable and in 1903 the building of a new pig house. Come the winter of 1905, and 40 tons of stones were grubbed at the back of the barn field. Eighty tons of stones were grubbed in the river garden and in February 1906, 30 tons were removed in the same laborious manner from the fallow garden.

In all of this Robert Miller had the help of his brother Edward and of his sons, Christopher and Edward, who were classified in the 1901 census as farm assistants. A servant boy or two may also have been involved. However, the main burden fell upon the head of household, 'a hardworking man,' if ever there was one. This is already demonstrable in his command over livestock husbandry. Numbers alone justify the point. Then there is also the discipline of his commitment to the tillage field as exemplified in programmed ploughing and harrowing to make the earth good for a crop. And he was an inveterate note taker, with his finger always on the pulse of life on the farm. A note is made of cows bulling and being bulled, with their names stated and the dates specified. It was the same with the serving of sows and mares. Comings and goings of the grass availing cattle of labourers or smallholders are also noted. For example, Patt Wingle brought three heifers to grass on 22 November 1898 and, having taken them away for 4 days, he brought them back again on 3 December. And a record of quarter ground allocations is still kept, which in the period 1897-9 included the name of Thomas McGrath of Kilscannell, whose grandaughter ultimately married a grandson of Robert Miller's.[5]

In those same late century years Robert was able to exploit the gravel workings on his farm as ballast for the Tralee branch of the Waterford, Limerick and Western Railway.[6] Coolybrown hill (215' O.D.) yielded the morainic deposits and hard work did the rest (fig. 15). In June 1896 the provision of ballast yielded £4.40; in March and October 1897, £9.74; in June 1898, £7.33; at another unspecified time, £7.70; and in May 1900, £4.03. Ballast was paid for at the rate of 1s.-4d. (6$^1/_2$ p.) per cubic yard and in all that is specified, the redoubtable Robert Miller and his men supplied some 511 cubic yards which they left alongside the rail, to be loaded into wagons.

There is no dearth of evidence of hard work therefore on the part of Robert Miller. Still for all that, life remained a struggle and equally in this area a sufficiency of evidence may be adduced. For example, on at least four separate occasions during the 1890s Robert Miller was faced with final rent demands from his landlord. He appears always to have paid under pressure. The same applied to credit with the suppliers

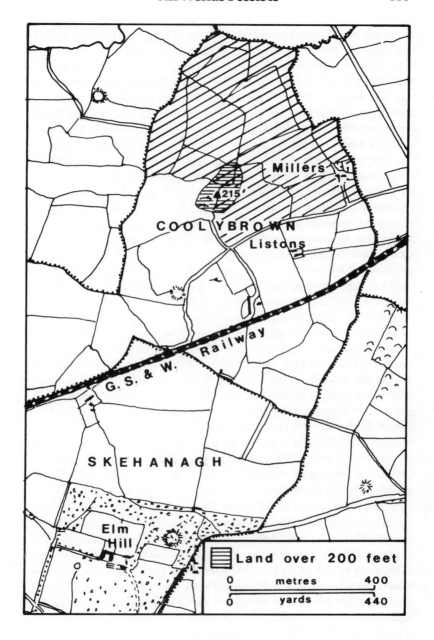

Fig. 15   The Miller farm in its local setting *circa* 1920

of goods and services. On 6 November 1896, for instance, he was issued with a final notice of fees due for the service of a stallion. The bill is marked paid on 14 November 1896. Availing fully of credit facilities but always paying their way was the norm with the Millers, and accounts were duly settled with a great diversity of interests in Rathkeale, Newcastle West and Limerick city. Sometimes it may have meant that loan facilities had to be taken up. In the period 1911-14, for instance, a whole series of notices for amounts of up to £10 issued from the Private Advance Bank at Catherine Street, Limerick, and it may also be pertinent to note the retention among the Miller papers of a newspaper advertisement relating to money lending from the Christmas of 1897.

Turning to his conduct of business, Robert Miller favoured Rathkeale more than Newcastle, although he was about equidistant from both. This is to judge by extant receipts. In Rathkeale there was McDonnells for the provision of clover, ryegrass fertiliser etc., David O'Shaughnessys for footwear, Hickeys for meat, Moylans for drapery, Hartigans for machine parts and Johnstones of Castlematrix mills for flour and meal. In Newcastle West there was Phelans for hardware, P.O'Shaughnessys for general merchandise, and Burtons and Fordes for drapery. Nearer home James Doody, the postmaster at Ardagh, was sometimes favoured with Bob Miller's custom, while in Limerick city the large agricultural concern of J.P. Evans & Co. was occasionally called upon for the supply of implements and seeds. Only fairs would have drawn him further afield and he was known to have once bought a horse at the fair of Killorglin which - because of the propensity of the animal to sit down under a cart - he did not keep long.

His lifetime commitment was to his farm of 53 statute or 33 Irish acres and he came through many vicissitudes to greet the day when his status changed from tenant under Maunsell to proprietor in his own right. Throughout the country as a whole a complex series of legislation was enacted to pave the way for tenant purchase,[7] while specifically in the case of the Maunsell estate the provisions of the Land Act of 1903 were adopted in making an offer to sell to the occupying tenants. This was in September 1908. The purchase money for the Miller farm was set at £753 which meant a reduction of 6s. (30p.) in the £ in the prevailing rent, to be paid by way of annuities over 21.54 years of the purchase. In making the offer Maunsell hoped to avoid any 'lingering negociations' and the agent acting on his behalf sought an immediate reply, since 'the preliminaries incidental to a sale take a long time to get through.' In the event, it took until 26 February 1914 before the farm on Coolybrown hill was vested in Robert Miller by fiat of the Irish Land Commission. Later on 23 October that same year he was registered as full owner. As a man of the land Bob had come through the most decisive transition of his life. At the age of 73 he at last owned the land he loved.

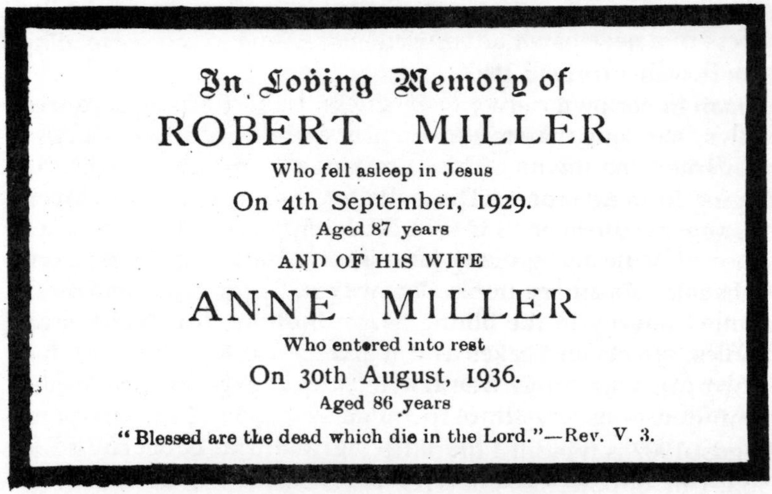

In Loving Memory of

ROBERT MILLER

Who fell asleep in Jesus

On 4th September, 1929.

Aged 87 years

AND OF HIS WIFE

ANNE MILLER

Who entered into rest

On 30th August, 1936.

Aged 86 years

" Blessed are the dead which die in the Lord."—Rev. V. 3.

Plate 13 Mortuary card of Robert and Anne Miller

However, he could scarcely enjoy his new proprietorial standing, having developed a bronchial condition which was to grow acute over time. Unable to go to bed, Old Bob, as he was known, spent his last years in a big armchair by the fire, covered in 'a big oul' shawl.' He was nursed all the way by his daughter Rosie, who slept in a bed beside him, and tended to her father through the long nights of illness. Then on the 3rd. day of September 1929 the old man asked to go to bed. He died the following day. On 6 September he was buried in the ancestral plot alongside the Holy Trinity Church, Rathkeale. He had reached the noble age of 88, one year more than he is credited with in his mortuary card (plate 13).

III

Plate 14
Still a formidable little woman in her
own right, Annie Miller *circa* 1930

Robert was survived by his wife Anne. A formidable little woman in her own right (plate 14), Annie as she was popularly known, had long maintained her own network of contacts. She frequented the towns of Newcastle West and Rathkeale, and judging from extant receipts, she like her husband, favoured the latter over the former. She kept a long-running account with the house of Mulcahy, grocery and spirit dealers, of Main Street, Rathkeale. Ordinary items such as tea, sugar, meat and soap counted heavily in the billing, while porter, whiskey, tobacco, candles, sweets and cakes also registered a recurring presence. Shopping was done weekly and a bill for once wrongly computed at 8s.-2$^1/_2$ d. (41p.) instead of 7s.-2$^1/_2$ d. (36p.) in August 1907 is typical: 1 qr. of tea 7$^1/_2$ d. (3p.), 1 qr. of sugar 7d. (3p.), 1 pt. of porter 2$^1/_2$ d. (1p.), 1 lb. of soap 3d. (1$^1/_2$ p.), cakes and sweets 1$^1/_2$ d. ($^1/_2$ p.), and 12$^1/_2$ lbs. of meat 5s.-5 d.(27p.).

She had recourse too to Newcastle West, from where a curious little snippet on wartime disruption came to her from the pen of Thomas Hartnett of Maiden Street, a motor and cycle manufacturer. It is dated 16 June 1915.

Dear Mrs. Miller, On account of the war I have still done nothing to the lady bicycle. But I have desired to fit more expensive tyres so that I may not disappoint you again. I am keeping you too long. 10/- or 15/- I know will not make much difference. So it will be ready and your girl may come and ride home. Hoping you will be pleased.

Whether she was or not, we do not know. What we do know is that the most abiding memory of her in Newcastle is on market day, taking tea with a friend in a local hostelry.

There was also a broad range of contact with her own people, among whom Annie was highly esteemed. An early undated letter from her Aunt Emily shows the cordiality of the relationship and the eagerness with which her visits were anticipated. Annie is asked to bring her melodeon along the next time. All she had to do is to come 'when the weather will be fine and we will have good times again.' The writer adds, but with scarcely any hint of admonition, that ' your goose is laying away still.' This was very much the stuff of correspondence among rural women within travelling distance of each other. It served to signal intending visits, report on family and friends, and comment on the behavioural pattern of fowl or the price of eggs.

There were letters too from her brother Jacob of Ballycahane and from her sisters Julia and Sarah. Jacob in a short undated note appears to be invoking Annie's help in arranging an introductory meeting between a young man and a young woman from their respective localities. Julia writes at a Christmas time to extend seasonal greetings and to express the hope that Annie would hear soon from her eldest son Christy who had emigrated to Australia. Sarah writes during the war years of 1914-15 with invitations to visit her at Garrenroe, reports on the visits of Annie's children, and the usual family news and enquiries. Reference to current events is restricted to a rhetorical question and a comment: ' Isn't the war terrible? Everything is so dear!' Years later in old age there is just the briefest of Christmas greetings from Sarah to her sister Annie.

However, that same Christmas there is a much more substantial piece from further afield. It comes from the pen of Elizabeth Preston Brawn, or Lizzie Preston as she would have been known back home.[8] Writing from Lowell in Massachusetts on 5 December 1934, Lizzie renews an old friendship.

> My dear cousin Annie, I dont know who owes a letter. But I think it is you — I think so few of us left, we ought to keep in touch. Uncle Robert Delmege died,[9] also Aunt Louie[10] in Australia. I wrote to Killeheen, Reens.

She then inquires after Annie's family, before going on to recount the successes of her own.

> How is Barbara and family? How many has she? also Mary Anne, Rosabel and Clara and the boys. Poor Emily, but better off! I have a son married since August. Francis got a

fine wife. They were married August 4th '34. Her name
was Goldie Bubier. They seem quite happy. So I had one
busy summer, Francis getting married and Billie graduated
from the M.S.C. and is no[w] teaching commercial law.
Evelyn is in Fla., also doing well. So God has been very
good [to] them all.

In turning from the familial to the general, however, she reports
that 'America is in a deplorable condition,' with so many idle
and no let up in the great depression.

Next she poses questions about her Delmege ancestry because,
like many an emigrant, she was keen to renew old world
genealogies.

Can you tell me how many brothers and sisters my
grandfather Delmege had and what his father's and
mother's names were? It seems awful to think we know so
little of our folks. I will be grateful. Recently in an exam the
question was: Name grandparents, both sides, and relations.
Was not cousin Robert's mother (your husband's mother) a
Delmege?
You knew Mary Doyle was dead. She was mother's sister.
She left three boys. One is married here in Lowell [and] was
home twice to Ireland from U.S.A.

As Mary Anne Delmege before she married, Mary Doyle had
herself written to Annie with great affection way back in the
1880s. Clearly her son had kept up the love for Ireland!

Seasonal greetings then give way to nostalgia as Lizzie
lovingly recounts old times and unlocks the intimacies of the
neighbourhood of Ardagh (fig. 16).

I hope you spend a pleasant Xmas and would like to be
there to eat a duck egg with you. [I] may some day visit,
when times get settled. I often think back of the times we
had together - Go to Rathronan to church - over to
Cahermoyle - and to Massey's place - Was it Glenville? Saw
recently in *Times* New York where one of the Masseys of
Stone Ville died. I would like to see you all. You and
grandma were always good to me.

There are questions for Annie's daughter Barbara as to whether
she considered the writer fat and whether any of the Odells
were still resident in Mount Pleasant, Askeaton.[11] Longingly
and in conclusion Lizzie adds, 'if I was there our tongues would
run!'

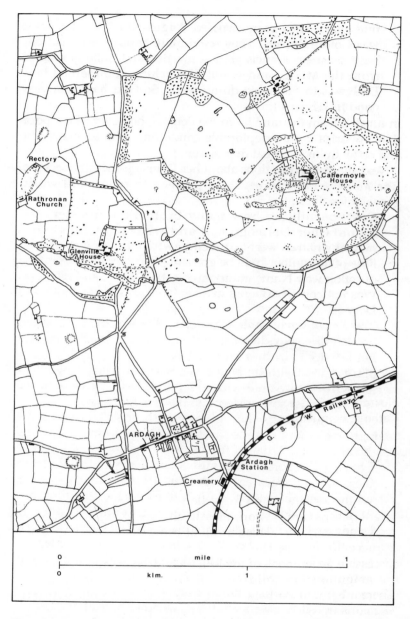

Fig. 16   Unlocking the intimacies of the neighbourhood of Ardagh,
Elizabeth Preston Brawn in a letter home at Christmas

There was certainly much to talk about at a time when the recipient was well into her eighties, and still sprightly. Indeed Annie's sprightliness may well have counted against her, as she fell while chasing a pig round the yard and broke her hip. She was able to carry on for some time with the aid of a crutch, but increasing debility gradually took its toll. She died on 30 August 1936. W. Ruttle of Nantenan, Askeaton, was appointed undertaker and the next day she was laid to rest alongside her husband Robert. Her funeral expenses amounting to £10.50 were paid in full two days later.

Old Annie Miller is remembered warmly in the neighbour-hood of Coolybrown and the following tribute by Jim Scanlan from nearby Rathreagh serves to recount the life of a good and kindly and humorous woman. This was in the course of a letter of sympathy to her daughter Rosie, dated 22 September 1936.

> Your dear mother had a grand record. Besides rearing and bringing up a large and respectful family, a good wife and mother, she was respected and beloved by all the neighbourhood and all who came into contact with her. I often recall the fun and laughter she made when visiting our house with your dear deceased father, and as times were hard and trying, they went through life nobly. Your dear mother spent a long and useful life and may she rest in peace in eternity.

No more needs to be added to this glowing tribute from a Catholic neighbour.

IV

Indeed the Millers got on marvellously well with their Catholic neighbours, among whom they lived as a kind of one-family Protestant enclave. This no doubt came about through long-term residence in the same townland and also through successive generations of the Miller children mixing freely with the neighbouring children in local schools. The family of Christopher and Barbara Miller had gone to the old school in Rathgoonan, while that of Robert and Anne attended the old school at Coolcappagh (see fig. 3). Both were Catholic in ethos and the only sundering to occur came at the times appointed for religious instruction. Otherwise they all stayed together, with the lasting consequences of warmth and conviviality that shines through in the Miller correspondence.

Picking up specifically on the children of Robert and Anne, if we take the 1901 census as base line, we find four of them still at school. Rosie was then aged 14, Clara 13, Robin 11 and John Albert 6. All with the exception of John Albert were literate and numerate. Young Jack could only read at that stage. Four of the older children had remained at home, along with their parents and uncle Ned. Emily aged 21 and Mary Anne aged 19 both fell into the classification of farmer's daughter, for whom either service or marriage or perhaps emigration was in prospect. The two remaining boys, Christopher aged 18 and Edward aged 16, helped out on the farm. They each merited the rank of farm assistant. Barbara alone was missing from the household, and with good reason.

Plate 15
Barbara Ruttle née Miller at home in Liffane

She had married the previous year. On 26 September 1900 she approached the nuptial altar of Rathronan Church and came away the bride of Michael James Ruttle, a farmer from the townland of Cloonreask near Askeaton. It was an event much celebrated on the day and for several days afterwards, and it came to be recounted as 'the wedding of Coolybrown.' The billing appears justified as the bride was a strikingly handsome woman and the first of her family to marry (plate 15). She was subsequently to face many trials, one of the earliest of which was to lose the farm at Cloonreask[12] and be relocated at Liffane, where her husband worked for forty years as general manager to the landlord family of Hewson. She was also to rear a family of twelve children; George, Albert, Bob, twins Willie and Christopher, Ned, Emily, Violet, Bessie, Annie, Lil and John. Her son Willie remembers her lovingly as he recounts the days when up to forty children would play hurling in the big field in

Liffane and his mother would treat them all to the best of homecooking afterwards.

Barbara's sisters, Emily and Mary Anne, both followed her example by marrying farmers of their own religious persuasion, but only after considerable intervals had elapsed. Indeed Emily struck up the same Palatine clan connection as her older sister by marrying Henry Ruttle of Ballyengland, Askeaton, on 23 July 1912. Ruttle was a big farmer but fond of the drink, and poor

Plate 16 Mary Anne Miller

Plate 17 Clara Miller

Emily had a short life with him. She bore two children, Bobby and Willie, but then died tragically without giving birth to a third. Mary Anne fared much better. She married Willie Gardiner, a strong farmer from the Ballyclough area of Co. Cork and a nice man to boot. They were wed in the Holy Trinity Church, Rathkeale, on New Year's Day 1918. In her early years of marriage Mary Anne complained of loneliness to her sister Clara, but she was kept busy with a 6 a.m. rising, her routine household chores and what she deemed the customary practice of plucking two duck on a Friday for Sunday dinner. Later her children - Jane Anne, Bobby and especially Dolly - were among the most active correspondents to the old home in Coolybrown.

Viewed by her aunt Sarah of Garrenroe as 'a real nice girl,' Clara was the youngest of the Miller sisters and the last of them to marry. She spent many years in domestic service while carrying on a long-running courtship with Jeremiah Mulcair, a big farmer from Aughinish Island, before eventually marrying him in the 1920s (plate 18). This was a mixed marriage, with all of the attendant problems and traumas created by Church decree. Among the most poignant was the occasion of the first communion of the couple's only child, Jimmy, when his Protestant mother could not present him along with all the other children. Instead it fell to a neighbour, Mary Anne Dundon and her daughter Bridgie, to bring young Jimmy along to the local church. As for Jerry Mulcair, he appears - certainly in the early days - to have been well regarded by the Miller household of Coolybrown, from where Clara's sister Rosie wrote to him on 4 November 1928.

Plate 18 Jerry Mulcair and Clara Miller on their wedding day

I had a notion this time past in going to see ye. I missed you greatly this year for September visit. I would thank you very much to drop me a line to let me know how both [of] ye are. Must close. With tons of love from mother and all, and accept the same from myself. Father is nicely. Write soon. Give my love to Clara.

Two of Mulcair's own letters to Rosie are also extant from August 1930, detailing Clara's improving state of health, and asking for a visit as well as promising one.

However, when it comes to remembrance, Clara - who used to

accompany her husband annually to the Puck Fair of Killorglin -
is the one regarded with warmth and affection. She and Mary
Anne Dundon were great friends. Together they often visited
the Miller home in Coolybrown: one such occasion being
signalled in advance by letter when Mrs. Dundon's son, P.J.,
would drive them up of a Sunday in his hired car. Clara was a
wonderful cook. Warned when young 'not to forget her
cooking,' clearly she never did, and she was most generous in
sharing the fruits of her culinary endeavours. Out-of-doors she
was a superb gardener. She caught all of the glorious
informality of the Palatine garden, with the interspersing of
shrubs and flowers and the apparently spontaneous creation of
height, tone and colour. An especially prized possession was a
vinegar plant unique to the locality. It reflected the uniqueness
of the woman herself.

V

Like their uncles before them, two of the Miller boys took to the
emigrant trail. At the age of 28, Christy the eldest of them, had
made a start for Australia, something that was picked up in the
grapevine at Ballycahane. Such is evident in a letter dated 7
October 1910 from Dora Miller to one of her cousins in
Coolybrown.

> Is it true that your brother Christ[y] has gone to Australia?
> We heard it here but did not quite believe it, as we t[h]ought
> he would come around here to say goodbye before he left.

Neither did Christy produce anything that remains extant from
his early Australian days and the first we learn of him comes by
way of a standard hospital admissions card issued by Army
Field Service in October 1918. It subsequently transpires that
this man of Coolybrown was a member of the 12th Army Field
Artillery Brigade attached to the Australian Imperial Force. As
such he may well have seen action in the first World War.[13]
Whether as a consequence he was sick or wounded, is
undisclosed. The only other available report states his condition
to be stationary. This was on 12 November 1918, the day after
the war officially ended.

Later Christy Miller was able to pick up the threads of civilian
life in Australia, where he was joined *circa* June 1920 by his
brother Jack, the youngest of them all. This is to judge from a

later letter home to sister Rosie. Also judging from subsequent correspondence, it is clear that the two Miller brothers spent the bulk of their Australian days together. All but one of the extant letters comes from the pen of Jack and the earliest hailed from c/o Brown Coal Mine Post Office, Gippsland, Victoria. Dated 15 June 1923, it is addressed to his sister Rosie at Coolybrown.

> In answer to your welcome letter, I was very pleased to hear from you, and that yea are all quite well, as this leaves me at present, thank God. I was very sorry to hear of Dan Corbet[t]'s death.[14] Old Mrs. Mack was no surprise as she lived to be a ripe old age. I was very pleased to hear father and mother put in the winter well. I see by the papers things are getting very cheap in the old country again. I suppose the farmers miss their big prices. I should think their creamery cheques would be getting small. I see in to-day's paper the Australian government is going to rea ship their butter home from London. They can get a better price for it. I was surprised to hear of John Miller's short time in God's own country. Perhaps he arrived here in summer time and the heat fed him up.

Unlike Jack himself, his cousin did not take to Australia. The Ballycahane man took to America instead.[15]

Turning to his own time in Australia, Jack appears relieved to have forsaken the backcountry of New South Wales.

> I left New South Wales early in January. There was a bad drought on there. How as ever, I wasn't sorry to leave the back country and drift to a bit of civilisation. I enclose two snapshot photograph[s] I got taken in the bush when I was in NSW. One was my home for 18 months and the other is myself and one of my big dogs. I will send you my photo when I get to the city to get it taken. Christy is here with me. He told me he wrote home recently.

Both the Miller brothers subsequently went to the city to have their photographs taken. In Whitney Bros. Electric Studios at 118 Bourke Street, Melbourne, they posed individually for the camera and, dressed in their best, these handsome men appear determined to cut a dash back home. In portraiture as in life, the Millers acquitted themselves well (plates 19 and 20).

One other topic merited mention in the letter. This related to the property blocks in Albany which came to be transferred to Rosie Miller after the death of her uncle Ned. Obtaining probate

Plate 19 Christopher Miller,   Plate 20 Jack Miller,
          Melbourne, *c.* 1923   Melbourne, *c.* 1923

and seeking a valuation thereafter proved a protracted business,
with three firms of solicitors - one in Rathkeale, Ireland, and two
in Perth, Western Australia - acting in the matter. On 18 August
1910 the property was reported as 'at present valueless and
would not realise the cost of obtaining probate, but would
probably become of some value should Albany improve.'
Clearly Rosie continued to be solicitous about her bequest and
had asked Jack to inquire into it on her behalf.

> Well dear Rosie, as regards your property, I intend to have a
> look at them some day. But not to dishearten you, I am told
> Albany is a pretty small town. But apart from all that, I will
> have a look for myself some time, and to see if it is a gold
> chain or a white horse!

The latter ultimately appears to have been the case and uncle
Edward Miller's early optimism was never really vindicated.

Jack's next available communication comes on 5 November
1927. In it he extends Christmas greetings to all at home and he
writes on this occasion to Rosie from St. Andrew's Place,
Sydney.

> I received your letter and paper to-day. I was very pleased
> to hear yea are all quite well. We had a very dry spell here.
> Sheep was dying in millions. But the drought broke. We
> got a general rain. The grass grow[s] very quick here after
> rain. During the drought one could have bought sheep for
> 3d. per head. When the rain came they jumped up to £1 per
> head.

On a familial note, both Christy and himself were very sorry to hear that their Dad was getting such poor health and in the wider context of home Jack's ' best of remembrance' was conveyed to all inquiring friends and neighbours.

For the next of his extant communications, we find that Jack and Christy Miller had moved decisively inland to Mitta Junction, via Wodonga, in Victoria. This was on 14 June 1932 when the great depression was still casting a giant shadow across the world stage.

> The big financial depression seems to hang on. The Australian pound is still very low in London. New Zealand is in a very bad way. The unemployed nearly pulled down all the towns, rioting for food. Primary produce is very cheap here. I seen eggs retailed @ $6^1/_2$ d. [3p.] per doz. and potatoes @ £4 per ton.

With currency and commodities at such a low ebb and food scarce, the very fabric of society was under threat.

However, Jack's own mood perks up as he contemplates his time in Australia and the attractions of its climate.

> This present month I have 12 years colonial experience. I am pretty well climatised now. The climate of Australia is much different to what it is in Ireland. It is mid winter here now, and [we] get nice sunny days. In a big country like this, when one get[s] inland the weather is very calm, [with] very little wind for about nine months of the year. Around where I am living oranges and lemons are grown in abundance.

Still whatever about this Mediterranean flavour, in the larger setting around Wodonga pasture for sheep and cattle constituted the predominant land use.[16]

To finish, Jack focuses upon a significant political transition at home, with the assumption of power by the DeValera- led government of 1932.

> I see by the papers yea got a very staunch new government. I see the president is putting up a good fight to pay John Bull by the mile. I should think it would be a big item to Ireland to get the land annuities cancelled.

Within a few months of taking power the new government was embroiled in economic war with Britain following on from DeValera's withholding of the land annuities. Such were payable under the legislation that had made landowners of

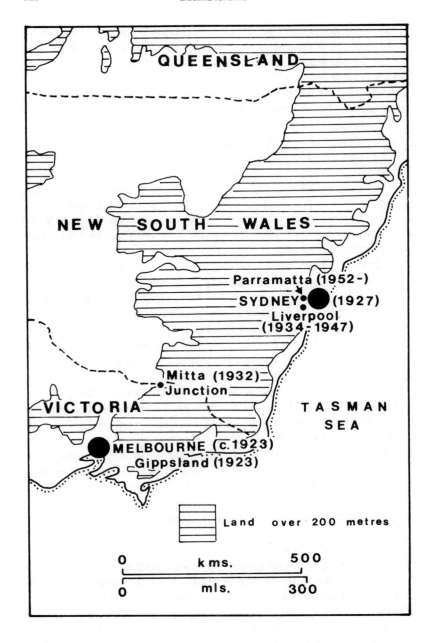

Fig. 17   The Australian sphere of Jack and Christy Miller

former tenants and their cancellation would be warmly welcomed by a man like Jack Miller who was born to the land under the old regime.

Jack's next letter comes some two years later when he and Christy had again shifted ground decisively to the Liverpool area of New South Wales, some 20 miles south west of Sydney. The financial depression still hung over Australia, with concomitant hard times for the farmers and cheap prices for their products. However, the essential thrust of Jack's letter is personal.

> Well dear Rosie, I may as well tell you I am getting very poor health for the past few years. I got a very bad attack from rheumatism this year. I was crippled right up from it. I could scarcely move a hand or foot with it. About two years ago I nearly went under with it. The only thing that saved me [was that] I happened to get to a good hospital. I am better again. I can nearly walk about as good as ever. But it left me with a very weak heart. I was thinking of going home to yea. If I was to go, it would be for to stay. It would be a good idea for you to consult the new boss[17] on the matter, and let me know what he thinks of the move.

The only other news concerned Christy who still stayed along with Jack. He is reported as being 'in the pink of condition,' having gone on the day of writing, to Sydney for a holiday.

Only once more do we hear from Jack. This was on 10 June 1936 when he acknowledges a time-lag in writing home to Rosie. His address is the same as before.

> I would have wrote to you before now, but I was away out west doing a bit of droving. Well Rosie, I suppose yea was disappointed as I did not go home. I got a lot better in health. Medical advice would not be keen in changing climate for me just for a while, and then of course the exchange rate is going up to 35% again. That means one would lose £35 out of every hundred.

For Jack, going home no longer appears a viable option.

In its stead he will content himself with news from home and he has pointers for Rosie on how to prepare a good informative letter.

> When writing again dont be in a hurry. Write a little bit each night and tell us all the ups and downs of the neighbourhood. A letter from home does be always very

welcome by everybody.
On that evocative note, Jack Miller takes his leave.

Thereafter there is a long gap before word reaches us on how the emigrant brothers are faring. Indeed the prolonged absence of a communication is noted by Rosie in the draught of a letter of 10 June 1946. She is most anxious to know if there is any news of them. In the event, the last account from either one of them to survive comes to her in a letter from Christy of 15 September 1947. It is addressed from Turner Avenue, West Hoseton P.O.. via Liverpool, NSW, which indicates a measure of residential stability on the part of the writer for 10 to 12 years. However, in other respects things had changed, especially for Jack who was now hospitalised.

> I had been to see Jack on the 10 September 1947. He seem[s] to be [a] little better looking. Well he get[s] changes, some good and [some] bad. He got your letter. You can be expecting one from him.

Whether such a letter came or not is problematic. Much less so was Jack's continuing status, since he was to spend the rest of his life in the mental hospital at Parramatta near Sydney. He was still there in 1952 when the medical superintendent reported him in good physical health, happy and contented, but also delusional, and occasionally restless and talkative.

As for Christy, he too was destined to live out his life in Australia. At the time of writing he could not contemplate the demands of the Irish climate, and although then able to proclaim good health, he was to die within the year. The settlement of his affairs shows that he had kept fowl, as well as a cow and a horse. His property realised £1,000 upon sale, and he had over £800 in bank deposits and commonwealth bonds worth £100. Shares worth £212.37$\frac{1}{2}$ each were awarded to all other family members, except Jack who was hospitalised and Emily who was already dead.[18] However, when the windfalls eventually reached the recipients in Ireland in September 1950, the recollection is that they had relatively little to get. Legal costs and complications had made small work of a tidy estate.

VI

Three of the Millers - Ned, Rosie and Robin - remained at home.

Plate 21
Ned Miller in his heyday at Coolybrown

They saw their parents die and their own life chances slip away. Indeed Ned in his advancing years once volunteered to a neighbour that he 'should have been given a kick up in the arse' when he was young to supply the necessary propulsion for marriage. He was a fine looking man and he certainly had his chances (plate 21). Rosie too had her admirers, when young and attractive (plate 22). Among them was Jack Shaughnessy from around Askeaton. However, apart from anything else her father's long illness ensured that she was kept at home to nurse him. As for Robin, he was a quiet and gentle person who once played the part of best man at a wedding, but was never destined to be the groom. By all three staying on at home on a farm, which by custom and practice was deemed one and indivisible, they spoiled each other's marriage chances. Moreover, Ned and Rosie were past the age of forty by the time their old father died. Upon their mother's death in 1936, the Miller trio - Ned, Rosie and Robin - were aged 51, 49 and 46 years respectively.

Plate 22
A camera-shy Rosie Miller *circa* 1920

Mediating in years and in gender, Rosie was linchpin in the household. This much is clear from incoming correspondence of a family nature, of which she was the sole recipient (fig. 18). It is to her, for example, that all the Australian letters are

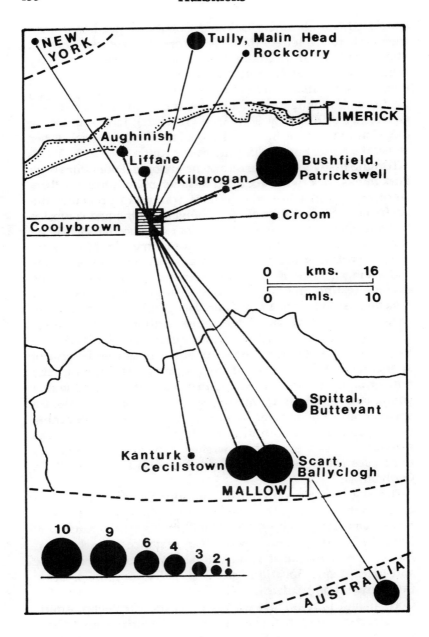

Fig. 18   Letters to Rosie, 1923–1956

addressed from brothers Jack and Christy. From her women friends there are letters from New York, from Rockcorry, Co. Monaghan, and from Malin, Co. Donegal. Her sisters, Mary Anne and Clara, also wrote on occasion, as did her nephews, John Ruttle of Liffane and Bobby Gardiner of Scart, Ballyclough, Co. Cork. Counting most of all, however, were the letters of her nieces, especially Dolly Shire (née Gardiner), Jane Ann Deane (née Gardiner) and Annie Cambridge (née Ruttle), as well as her namesake Rosie, Emily Cliffe and Bessie Ruttle.

Turning firstly to old friends and neighbours, Pollie from New York thinks back to the good old days when both their mothers were alive and when she herself was trying to meet the boyfriends. She asks fondly for Coolybrown hill and confesses that she often gets a longing for the old country, before adding stoically 'well such is life!' From Rockcorry, Co. Monaghan, Winnie Switzer writes of a Christmas time, again nostalgically, and asking if Rosie is still on the single list like herself. She extends festive greetings to all and in particular asks to be remembered to Robin. From Malin Head in Co. Donegal, Agnes writes on three occasions to sympathise with Rosie on the losses of her brother Christy (1948) and her sisters Barbara (1949) and Mary Anne (1954). On the fourth she dreads the thought of spending the Christmas of '53 amongst strangers in the northernmost recesses of the country, although married with a young family. She has a hankering after the carefree days she spent about Coolybrown. However, with an air approaching resignation she will admit 'well them days are gone!' She extends, as always, her best wishes to Ned and Robin, and expresses the hope that she and Rosie will meet again in Coolybrown.

Turning to correspondence from kin, the great bulk of it concerns the ordinary everyday exchanges that passed between related farm families in the 1940s and 50s, especially those who lived within relatively easy visiting distance of each other. Rosie's sphere extended at most to about 30 miles from home and took in such locations as Scart, Ballyclough, Co. Cork; Cecilstown, Lombardstown, Co. Cork; Spittal, Buttevant, Co. Cork; Bushfield, Patrickswell, Co. Limerick; Kilgrogan, Adare, Co. Limerick; Aughinish, Borrigone, Co. Limerick; and Liffane, Askeaton, Co. Limerick (fig. 19). Her married sisters had staked out the ground initially; later her married nieces amplified upon it. Rosie was especially kind to her nieces. Therefore acknowledgement features prominently for all that she sent: the boxes of plums from the home orchard, the lbs. of tea during wartime scarcity, the hankies and bows for the children at Christmas, the sweets and the biscuits at Christmas and at other times, and the cash contributions, including one for £10. In return there were visits or the promise of them, which were oftentimes circumscribed by the needs of the cow.

> Well Auntie, I intend to call back to see ye on Sunday after dinner just for a small chat, as we must be home for the cows. Our boy don't come on Sundays.

Another letter opens and closes with gratitude for 'the day we had with ye' and the hope is expressed that there would be 'many more days to meet again with God's help.'

Family and neighbourhood concerns mingle easily with news of the weather, livestock, crops and fowl. In particular, among rural women, there are exchanges about the last.

> My fowl are laying well. I have 5 ducks laying. [Eggs are] 4/- a dozen now in town. It was a pity the fox took so many of the hens.

In this area news was sometimes imparted with eagerness.

> Well now, I must tell you how many chickens I had. I had 4. I would have more only a goose went in on top of the hen a few days before they came out and crushed the eggs. But, however, the 4 are hardy and like hens.

There is also reference to exchanges of breeding stock.

> I meant to go back to you with the cock, but we were so busy with the corn. We got it threshed two weeks ago — Your cock and drake are doing fine. Hope yours is alright too. Eggs got more plentiful with me. I got 5/6 [27½ p.] a dozen in town this week.

And there are questions as well as reportage.

> Have you any chickens? I have some early ones. I have very little goslings, only 3 this year. The most of the eggs were bad.

Turkeys were always a difficult proposition.

> I did not sell the turkeys yet. The price is poor this year. I think I wont go in   for them the coming season. A couple of pigs would be better and easier.

On the whole, egg money was a valuable supplement to family income. Thus the vagaries of fowl animated the lives of the women who tended to them.

Sometimes, in the area of livestock, a niece of Rosie's would write to the Millers on behalf of her husband.

> He wants to know have ye a good ram lamb to sell later on. We have to sell mostly all our sheep. They are jumping into every field and into some of the neighbours. We only bought the ram last year, so we must sell him again. He was very lucky with one he bought before from ye. He would like one again from honest people. You can let me know.

The Millers were renowned for their probity. Therefore they could be counted upon to supply a reliable animal for sale, either privately, or at the horse and cattle fairs of Rathkeale and Newcastle West.

Everything of a written nature was mediated through Rosie. Not alone did she write on behalf of the family, she also kept notes relating to the doings of the farm and the comings and goings thereon. All the cows were bestowed with names, while their 'times' were duly noted. In the listing of 1947, for example, these mistresses of the pasture were known by the appellations of blue cow, white cow, speckled cow, pollie cow, young pollie cow, black Kerry cow and Ardagh cow. Sometimes they were known by the family from which they were acquired, such as Corbett's cow, Ruttle's cow or Liston's cow. Taken together, they betokened the significance of milk in the farm economy and to lend attestation on a daily basis, there was the round of creamery going to Ardagh, some three miles away. As well, the Millers were conspicuous orchard people. This is well seen in Rosie's 'account of an orchard' in the period 1945-9 when the produce realised £30.70, £8.62, £14.17$^{1}/_{2}$ and £20.05. Considering that a servant boy could then be employed for £10 or £12 a year, this puts receipts from the fine orchard behind the Miller house into some kind of perspective.

Indeed the servant boys still came and went, and Rosie kept track of them.

> Year 1937. Mikie Walsh has commenced service with me since first March. He worked with me till the 10th of March. He left then till 19th and worked 19th. £1 paid for March. May 1st, paid £1-5 for April. 2nd June, paid £1-5 for the month of May. 29th June, paid £1-5. July 17th, 8/- for insurance. Paid £1-5, 2nd of September, paid for the month of August. 27th September, £1-5 paid. Oct 30, paid £1-5.

Nov., £1-5 paid. Dec., 12/6 paid. 12/6 [62¹/₂ p.] insurance paid in full.

Plate 23 Robin and Ned Miller *circa* 1950

While Rosie kept account, Ned appears to have been the paymaster, as Daniel Costello duly acknowledges on 23 December 1936. Costello worked for the Millers in the years 1935-7. Others to do so during the 1940s and 50s were their near neighbours, the Bustons, who included Tony (1945) and Pat (1948-51).

In her advancing years Rosie Miller was to see many transitions, especially those which pertained to the mortality of her own family. To start, her brother Christy was to die in 1948, within a year of reporting good health in his only extant letter from Australia. At around the same time, her eldest sister Barbara was in decline. Barbara's health status is described by one daughter as 'not too bad' in May 1947; another reports her as 'not well for some time,' adding that 'she should not be like that at her age.' Ultimately cancer was diagnosed and she died at home in Liffane in March 1949. She was aged 71. Her funeral cortège for the three miles from Liffane to Askeaton was a sight to behold, and in filial tribute, her remains were shouldered through the main street of the town, before coming to rest at the old parish centre.

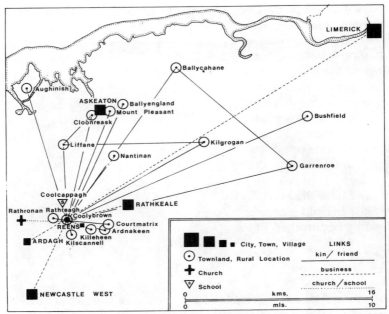

Fig. 19   The home county domain of the Millers of Coolybrown 1893-
1956

Later, another sister, Mary Anne Gardiner, suffered
deteriorating health as repeated heart attacks took a severe toll
on her. Towards the end the fear was expressed to Rosie that
'poor Mam won't do any good.' This was in January 1954 and
she died in the spring. In life she commanded the love and
devotion of her family, and the warmest of remembrances
afterwards.

> She was a good mother to us all. The home is very lonely
> without her. I always think of her. No doubt, her life on
> earth was an example of good living, piety and devotion to
> us all. She never said a bad word to me. May God comfort
> her.

The same attributes of good living, piety and devotion applied
to Clara Mulcair who nursed her husband through a protracted
illness till his death in 1947. Afterwards poor Clara suffered a
stroke, and although she was to live on for many more years,
her quality of life was greatly diminished.

Rosie kept in touch with them all. She was the homemaker at
Coolybrown, the linchpin of an ageing family. As such, she was

the key filter of family news. In her own right, she was a person of deep religious conviction; her sister Barbara had often asserted that ' no nun was as devout as Rosie.' Local renown as a lay preacher came her way and among the Miller memorabilia are the many little prayer books that bear her name. For her, life's quest is guided by scripture. She writes:

> Search the scriptures, for in them ye think ye have eternal life. The proof we love God is we go in to keep his commandments.

And she adds prescriptively:

> The wedding garment, clean hands, a pure heart and a holy life.

Rosie Miller died on 17 March 1956. On the night she was being waked her old sleeping place in front of the hearth was taken over by her brother, Robin. He filled the space till he died.

Epilogue

The farm passed to Ned Ruttle, a nephew, and has in turn passed on to Michael Ruttle, a grandnephew. Michael's father, Willie, still lights the hearth fire on winter days and the old farmstead that his mother, Barbara, came out of, is still kept up.[1]

I

The Millers of Coolybrown are remembered with affection. For three generations as farmers they had made their mark on the land and as a one-family Palatine enclave they had made their mark in the mind. They simply made a difference and the difference was there to be prized. And it was prized. They were nice people, decent people, honest, thrifty and hard-working. Terms such as these trip spontaneously off the tongue and the faces of old friends and neighbours light up in the act of recollection. They were the best of neighbours, giving of the fruit of their orchard, or obliging with a clutch of eggs for a

Plate 24 A lone apple tree where once there was an orchard

clocking hen or, on occasion, it might be a 'small bit of bacon', or
'a few lilies.' ' Go to them any day except Sunday!' ' They 'd do
nothing for you on Sunday' because they were absolutely
fastidious in their observance of the Sabbath.

Once on a Friday a tramp on his rounds came to the door and
Rosie welcomed him in. Although not bound by any rule of fast
or abstinence, the Millers used to eat eggs only on a Friday and
sitting the man down to table she put two fried eggs and a fine
feed in front of him. During the course of the meal Ned came in
from working in the fields. Somewhat startled at seeing the
dishevelled man eating his best at the table, Ned tacked a
question on to a comment. ' For a fine strappin' man like you,
how come you don't work?' The reply came with impeccable
candour. ' To tell you the truth, sir, I'm too lazy!'

Laziness was a word that scarcely entered the Miller lexicon,
never mind their mode of life. They were hard-working and
disciplined, fully committed to the culture of field and orchard,
and dedicated to the needs of their livestock. Like their
forefathers before them, they were innovators on the local scene,
being among the first to acquire a mowing machine and then
making themselves available to mow meadows for hire. They
were the possessors of an unusual breed of sheep - their animals
being long and distinctive - and if exotic influences were at
work, then we need think no further than their uncle Ned, back
from Australia. Consistent with all of this, the Millers rose very
early, and everyday they made the road to Ardagh first rattle to
the sound of creamery cans aboard their ass and cart. When
they got too old to go themselves, their neighbour Denis Liston
took the milk for them, along with his own, to Ardagh
creamery. However, the Millers lost none of their atavistic
traits, and invariably on a Sunday morning the Miller milk
would be landed in Liston's yard ever before the Listons had
risen from their beds.

Early rising meant an early dinner, sometimes at 11 a.m., but
usually at 11. 30. Then after eating they had a nap for a half an
hour or so. This was a practice they always adhered to, even
when saving hay or cutting corn. The old disciplines were
upheld therefore and bed at an appointed time counted among
them. An anecdote helps to illustrate the point. During the long
winter nights neighbours, who included Joe Liston, regularly
visited the Miller home. On one particular night the *craic* was

good and they stayed on late. Totally unannounced, the Millers started to drift away to their beds. Finally only Robin was left. He got up to go too, and as he did, he addressed his still seated guests with the words: ' Rake the fire, lads, before ye go and pull out the door!'

The Millers were different and they were adept at cultivating the difference, not least sartorially. The men always wore cravats and big wide peaked caps, and sometimes for riding, laced-up high boots and knickerbockers. Once the difference told in devastating fashion with Ned. He was out a day at ploughing, wearing wide khaki pants that became progressively frayed and folded over the course of the day, allowing bits of mud to get caught in the folds. Having finished his work in the evening, he rode over to Scanlans of Rathreagh. There he sat down by the fireside. One story proved good only until another was told and as the entertainment got all the time better, the particles of mud hardened like bullets with the heat of the fire. Riding home that night through a wild and weird place, Ned was sure he heard the sound of someone following him.

Plate 25 Another elegaic symbol visible from the old Miller home, Kilscannell Church in ruins

Whenever he stopped the sound stopped, only to start again whenever he rode on. He reached home in a state of utter desperation, covered in sweat. The poor man took to the bed immediately and spent several days there, before eventually discovering that the accumulations of a day's ploughing in unorthodox garb had come to unnerve him in the dark of night.

There was no denying the difference with the Millers. It showed again when their old mother died. The local women came to lay her out and help with entertaining the friends and relations who attended the wake, confident in the expectation that they would be there all night. They were very surprised therefore when Robin announced to the full house, ' If ye don't mind we'd like to take a rest and we'll let ye all go home.' With that, the Millers gently escorted their sympathisers to the door. They then put out the light and retired for the night. Such an early ending to a wake ran totally counter to the local tradition whereby mourners kept an all-night vigil in honour of the dead.[2] Thus in this respect as in others the Millers went their own quiet way.

II

Upholding a long cherished family tradition, the Millers were superb horsemen. Robin was known to sometimes ride on horseback to church service in Rathkeale, and occasionally to ride side-saddle on a big bay mare for his messages at Foleys of the Pike.[3] Ranging further afield he would ride over to Ruttles of Liffane, where his sister Barbara was married with a large family. Then he would entertain them all with tunes on the accordion, before returning home to Coolybrown. Upholding the Miller singularity, he is the very last man to be remembered locally who would saddle up his horse and ride off down the passage, and on by Ardagh, to the town of Newcastle West. Even in old age the love of riding stayed with him. He would mount an old donkey and move gently over the much loved fields of home.

Ned's love of horses took him annually to the famous race meeting in Listowel, Co. Kerry. On a late September day one year, Ned, in the company of Joe Liston and another man, set off as usual along the railway track to Ardagh station, some two miles away. The weather was atrocious, being both wet and stormy. Liston was a witty man and even on a bad day was not averse to taking a rise out of the company. Having stopped to take shelter at Liskilleen farm crossing, he ventured half seriously, ' Well aren't we the right eejits to think of going to Listowel on a day like this!' The other man said nothing, but Ned took the bait and looking at Liston with an odd kind of intensity he said, ' You 're quite right!' Then turning on his heel, he set off down the line back home. The other pair watched Ned go out of sight before continuing on to the station where they caught the race special, and with the benefit of a clearance, they proceeded to have a great day's racing in Listowel. Ned was never caught out again, but when he got old, he would close over the door on those same late September days and retire to the upper room. He could not bear to see the train in transit to the races.

The Millers of Coolybrown may be viewed culturally as hybrid figures and unlike, for example, a great many of their Palatine brethren - including all those of the Methodist persuasion - they showed no aversion to gambling. Robin, for his part, always bought a sweep ticket. He kept a half share himself and sold on two quarter shares to two neighbours. Once he created a sensation by drawing a horse under the pseudonym ' my big horse Coolybrown.' Unfortunately the horse was a non-starter, but even so the prize of £500 was a considerable sum in the Ireland of the late '30s or early '40s. On the occasion of the win one of the quarter shareholders had failed to pay up. He still got his share of the winnings.

Ned was the extrovert of the family and had a great liking for the game of pitch-'n-toss. He was regularly in attendance at the pitch-'n-toss school in Reens of a summer's evening and he might also have recourse afterwards to a similar school in Coolcappagh, where he struck up a cordial friendship with the Connors family. Ned was reputed to be a deadly pitcher. When in form, no one could get inside him, and being a master of body language ever before that term became fashionable, he cultivated a highly individualistic style of tossing, often with the most profitable results. One summer he had attempted on successive evenings to make a break for the Pike, only to be called back to chores that needed his attention. On the third evening, ' Miller' as he called himself, was determined to get away. He succeeded, much to the consternation of every other competitor in sight. Three days of starvation had made ' Miller' the hungriest and deadliest pitcher in the Pike.

The Millers also took a drink. Indeed they were well known through the conviviality of a drink at the Pike. Having recently posed of a man of Newcastle West, the question, ' Did you know the Millers of Coolybrown?,' he countered in the typically Irish manner, ' Didn't I drink porter with them in Reen's Pike!' At the fairs of Newcastle West, a Catholic farmer from Ballyine near the town used to say of them, again in the context of a congenial pub setting, ' They 'd be more with us than with their own crowd.' Ned used to head regularly for the Pike, and always on a Sunday night. He might call to Donovans, there to meet up with Tom Larkin, a farming friend of his, before making the short traverse to Foley's pub. Paddy Naughton, a blacksmith from Ardnakean, was a particular friend of Ned's at Foleys and much time would be spent discussing the kindred subjects that impinged upon the lives of farmers and blacksmiths. The half pint (of stout) was Ned's drink and whenever he came to buy he would call upon the publican by the name of ' Mister Michael.' In contrast with his older brother, Robin rarely stirred abroad to the pub at night. He might take a half pint in the daytime when calling for his messages and he'd be sure to have a drink the day of a fair.

The Millers of Coolybrown were well known too for their inventive turns of phrase. Again Ned, as the colourful extrovert, merits pride of place for phrasemaking. Once present in the company of Jack Teskey at a wake in the Palatine parent colony of Killeheen, Ned was far from enamoured of the proceedings when he discovered that there wasn't going to be a 'drop a' drink' in honour of the dead. However, his sense of humour triumphed over his sense of deprivation, and he described the event ever after as a ' wake spatter.' In contrast, Robin's inventiveness might stem from more solitary pursuits such as hunting through the fields, and whenever his pair of terriers would raise a rabbit, he would distil the excitement of the moment as ' a great rattle.' Both men were known for their old world courtesies. For instance, they would refer to their sister as ' Miss Rosie,' and they would tip the cap in the act of salutation. Ned called every man he met ' mister' and every woman ' miss' or ' missus.' He also deserves the last word on this subject since a favourite aphorism/ malapropism of his was, ' Talk is great if you could put your foot in it.'

For a pastime there was nothing Robin liked better than to take out the button accordion and play away to his heart's content of a summer's evening. He would sit in the horse car in the yard or he would go up onto the hill to find a congenial spot in which to play. He entertained not only himself but the whole neighbourhood with a repertoire which included the well known dance tune ' The Maids of Ardagh.' Ned, for his part, used to catch goldfinches, attracting those in the wild with a caged bird, about which he spread lime. In the manner of the time he kept the caged birds in the house and delighted in their singing. Once he stayed up all night with a bird that was pining. That same little singer was saved.

III

All around the neighbourhood there are evocations of the Millers of Coolybrown. Images re-surface in the mind and the eye may pick out Robin travelling the ' low road' aboard his horse and creeled car, destined with his few sheep, for the fair of Newcastle; or Ned walking the road by Kilreash of a Sunday, bound for Rathronan Church where, as sexton, he would ring out the bell of welcome; or Rosie on one of her rare expeditions to town in the ass and car, laden on the inward journey with eggs and the produce of the orchard. At home there was ever a welcome at the door from Robin, while Rosie could be counted upon to put a boiled egg and a feed of home-made niceties in front of any visitor; and Ned, for a young niece or nephew, might be persuaded to reveal the secrets of his sleeping place in what could pass in a child's mind as a hole in the wall.[4] They all came together to pray by the hearth, and when they got older they might miss service, but never prayer on a Sunday. Sequentially from Rosie to Ned to Robin they passed on to the rewards of eternity.[5] Ned died in 1962, the same year as his sister Clara Mulcair, and Robin passed away at the end of a noble line on 22 March 1969.

Evocations of the old Miller home still keep crowding in. A man now in his seventies takes on the mind of a boy as he

Plate 26 The old Miller home and the sentinel tree

recalls the delicious kitchen smells that greeted the visitor coming up the passage to the house. In particular, he recounts the succulent promise of chicken or rabbit roasting for the Sunday dinner. An emigrant in a now lost letter, recalls the smell of baking buns, and if she could only go back again for a few hours, everything with her world would be put to rights. Another visitor recalls going up of an evening in an old Morris Oxford car and seeing what he thought was a cock of hay in the middle of the yard. The Miller men had cut a hazel hedge and stacked the cuttings in the mode of a haycock, and whenever they wanted kindling, they took from the pile in the middle of the yard. Then towards the end, there are recollections of small windows admitting but little light, yet still cluttered with all kinds of knick-knacks, as the gathering gloom signalled the imminent demise of the Millers.

To-day the old *genius loci* hangs over Coolybrown hill, working its way up through the ash that flank the passage to the crowning sentinel tree. Come inside the still landlord-plated door. Sit on an old súgán chair. Take in the artefacts of hearth and horse. Feel the peace, savour the solitude, and think of the Millers of Coolybrown. For them all worlds were possible, including the mansions of heaven.

Notes and References

Introduction
1. Register of marriages, Kilscannell parish 1825–86, 17.
2. The dates of birth of the children of Christopher and Barbara are taken from the record preserved in the Miller family Bible.
3. Bestowal of the same Christian name was a common practice in such circumstances. See R. ffolliott, ' Irish naming practices before the Famine,' *The Irish Ancestor* 18, 1, 1986, 1–4.
4. See P.J. O'Connor, *People make places : the story of the Irish Palatines*, Newcastle West, 1989, 1–41, for a detailed reconstruction of the exodus of the Palatines from Germany in 1709 and their subsequent settlement in Ireland.
5. H. Jones, *The Palatine families of Ireland*, Camden, Maine, 1990, 84.
6 P.J. O'Connor, 'Palatine families on the Southwell estate 1709-12 to 1720,' *Irish Palatine Association Newsletter* 2, 1991, 9-15.
7. R. Renzing, *Pfälzer in Irland*, Kaiserslautern, 1989, 381.
8. Waterfield is described as a ' good old mansion ' in S. Lewis, *A topographical dictionary of Ireland* 1, London, 1837, s. v. Clounagh, 380.
9. The Miller-Bartman marriage maintained the web of Palatine interconnection, since Dora hailed from the secondary colony of Glenosheen in south east Limerick.
10. *Slater's national commercial directory of Ireland*, Manchester, 1846, s. v. Rathkeale, Co. Limerick, 305.

CHAPTER 1
1. Marginal note made by John Miller in road attendance/ account book dating between November 1846 and February 1850. John Miller died on 4 February 1853.
2. He is so described below the attendance record of men at work on the week ending 24 November 1849.
3. The idea of history being handed up rather than handed down now commands much greater attention than heretofore. It is seen at its best in the work of the great French historian, Fernand Braudel.
4. James Enright was a strong farmer in the townland of Skehanagh which adjoins Coolybrown. He held 107 acres of land valued at £80.25 and buildings valued at £2 *circa* 1850.
5. Michael Liston was a neighbour of the Millers in Coolybrown and a landless labourer. He lived in a house valued at 90 p. *circa* 1850.
6. Daniel was the son of George and Anne Eaton of Killeheen whose smallholding credentials are attested by the 3 acres of land they held there. Daniel was born on 29 January 1841.
7. See, for example, J. Lee, *The modernisation of Irish society 1848-1918*, Dublin, 1973, 9-11.
8. S. Clark, *Social origins of the Irish land war*, Princeton, 1979, 335.
9. P.J. O'Connor, 'Ireland's last best west : evidence from the Courtenay/ Devon estate,' *Journal of the Newcastle West Historical Society*, 1, 1990, 27.
10. This was where undertenants of the Millers cultivated their crops of potatoes and turnips on a seasonal basis.
11. The Miller farm was so described by Walter Ruttle, himself a Palatine farmer from the parent colony of Ballingrane in the parish of Nantenan.

12. The continuing humility of James Quaid's status is suggested by the 25 perches of land which he held under Christopher Miller in 1852-3. He lived in a house valued at 5s. (25p.).

13. P.R.O., London, HO, 184/5, 816. According to his service record, Christopher Miller, a Protestant from Co. Limerick, enlisted on 15 October 1847. He was 5' 8$^1/_2$" in height. Having received the recommendation of I. Studdert J. P., of Elm Hill, Kilscannell, he was allocated to the depot of Cork W. where he appears to have served until his resignation on 11 June 1855.

14. James Winter of Dromcolliher, parish clerk of the parish of Corcomohide, married Thirza Delmege of Killeheen, parish of Kilscannell, in Kilscannell parish church on 25 July 1836.

15. P.R.O., London, WO, 97/3468, 815. According to his service record Private Richard Miller embarked for India with his regiment on 31 December 1868 and landed there on 2 February 1869. Upon enlistment, his habits were accounted ' regular and temperate ' and his conduct ' very good.' He was 5' 11$^1/_8$" in height, with a fresh complexion, dark grey eyes and brown hair.

16. For a useful exposition on mobility as a characteristic of the Irish emigrant experience see, P. O'Farrell, *Letters from Irish Australia 1825-1925*, Sydney, 1984, 8 et passim.

17. Anne was the daughter of Jacob Miller of Ballycahane, Kilcornan parish, Kenry barony. According to the Griffith Valuation *circa* 1852, Jacob held 34 acres of land valued at £24.50 and 4 acres of bog valued at 20p. in the townland of Ballycahane. His buildings were valued at £2.80.

CHAPTER 2

1. Extract from Adam Miller's letter of 6 August 1853 to his brother Christopher Sr. at Coolybrown, requesting that his daughters Catherine and Anna be sent out to him in America.

2. B.S. Elliott, *Irish migrants in the Canadas - a new approach*, Montreal, 1988, 134-6.

3. W. Johnston, *The pioneers of Blanshard*, Toronto, 1899, 22-3.

4. C.A. Heald, *The Irish Palatines in Ontario : religion, ethnicity and rural migration*, (Gananoque: Langdale Press) forthcoming, 1994.

5. For an elaboration of the themes of pioneering life in Canada West see, C.J. Houston and W.J. Smyth, *Irish emigration and Canadian settlement : patterns, links and letters*, Toronto, 1990, espec. 241-86.

6. C.A. Heald, *op. cit.*, forthcoming.

7. *Personal Census 1861*, No. 1 Ward, township of Blanshard, entries 19-23.

8. F. McDonald and G. McWhiney, 'The Celtic South,' *History To-Day*, 30 July, 1980, 11-15; see also F. McDonald, ' The ethnic factor in Alabama history : a neglected dimension,' *Alabama Review* 32, 1978, 256-65; and F. McDonald, ' Cultural continuity and the shaping of the American South ' in E.D. Genovese and L. Hochberg (eds.), *Geographic perspectives in history*, Oxford, 1989, 215-34.

9. D.H. Akenson, ' Reading the texts of rural immigrants ; letters from the Irish in Australia, New Zealand and North America,' *Canadian papers in rural history* 7, 1990, 387-406.

10. This is an apparent reference to the 150 acres which her father and family owned in Alabama.

11. The aunt referred to is Barbara Miller, wife of Christopher, of Coolybrown.

12. According to Miller in his monumental study of Irish emigration to North

America, 'acute homesickness pervaded the letters and journals of most post-Famine emigrants.' However, the small sample of letters which underpins this study shows nothing of the kind. Ann Miller's state of 'acute homesickness' appears to have been uniquely her own among the correspondents to Coolybrown. See K.A. Miller, *Emigrants and exiles : Ireland and the Irish exodus to North America*, Oxford, 1985, 512.

13. See R. Rees, *New and naked land : making the prairies home*, Saskatoon, 1988, 94.

14. Born on 2 March 1857, Mary Anne was the daughter of the farming family of Jacob and Eliza Delmege of Killeheen. Located in the parish of Kilscannell, Killeheen was one of the parent Palatine colonies.

15. D.R. Meyer, ' The national integration of regional economies, 1860-1920, ' in R.D. Mitchell and P.A. Groves (eds.), *North America : the historical geography of a changing continent*, London, 1987, 344.

16. Sarah was married to William Gibbings gent., of Kilscannell, where four of their children were born in the period 1870-79.

CHAPTER 3

1. Extract from Christopher Miller's letter of 10 May 1859, written from the address of Knysna Main Station, in which he outlines his role as road overseer through *terra incognita*.

2. G.B. Dickason, *Irish settlers to the Cape*, Cape Town, 1973, 25 et passim.

3. D.H. Akenson, 'Reading the texts of rural immigrants : letters from the Irish in Australia, New Zealand and North America,' *Canadian papers in rural history* 7, 1990, 388-9; also P.O'Farrell, *The Irish in Australia*, Kensington, NSW, 1987, 54-8.

4. Mr. Maunsell, the landlord of Coolybrown, lived at Ballywilliam, Rathkeale.

5. The older name for Long Street was Derde Berg Dwarsstratt. Assuming that she remained *in situ* we should expect Mrs. Switzer to show up there in the Cape Town street directory of 1867. See L.G. Green, *Tavern of the seas*, Cape Town, 1947, 78, 85. However, during the summer of 1993 an exhaustive search of the 1867 directory and of earlier directories and almanacs failed to reveal any trace of the same Mrs. Switzer.

6. D.H. Akenson, *Small differences : Irish Catholics and Irish Protestants 1815-1922 - an international perspective*, Montreal, 1991, espec. 42-85.

7. This is surely the town of George, located about midway between Cape Town and Port Elizabeth, and only some 30 miles west of Knysna Main Station.

8. Kaffraria (from the Arabic Káfir "infidel") was the generic term applied by the Portuguese to all the territories along the south east coast of Africa. It became applied more specifically in the nineteenth century to those lands inhabited by the Xhosa-speaking peoples of the Transkei and Ciskei. In 1847, during the Cape frontier wars, the British government annexed the territory between the Keiskama and Kei rivers as the crown colony of British Kaffraria. From 1857 this area was opened up to white settlement - hence Christopher Miller's role as road overseer shortly thereafter! It was finally incorporated by a reluctant Cape Colony in 1865.

9. These were the Mfengu who belonged to the Ngqika group of Xhosa-speaking peoples and who along with the Thembu historically occupied the territory between the Keiskama and Kei rivers.

10. Although now considered pejorative, Kaffir or Caffer was used in the

nineteenth century as a synonym for Xhosa.

11. Khoi or Khoikhoi is the preferred term for people referred to in the older literature as 'Hottentots,' members of Late Stone Age herding communities whom the Cape Dutch first encountered in the seventeenth century.

12. F.J. Turner, ' The significance of the frontier in American history,' *American Historical Association Annual Report*, 1894, 199-227.

13. See, for example, H.P. Simonson, *Beyond the frontier : writers, western regionalism and a sense of place*, Fort Worth, 1989, 22.

14. M. Legassick, ' The frontier tradition in South African historiography,' in S. Marks and A. Atmore (eds.), *Economy and society in pre-industrial South Africa*, London, 1980, 44-79.

15. *Ibid.*, 45-6.

16. See A.J. Christopher, *Southern Africa: an historical geography*, Folkestone, 1976, 114-5.

17. For a review of the agricultural and pastoral frontier from *circa* 1860, see *ibid.*, 116-51.

18. T. Kirk, ' The Cape economy and the expropriation of the Kat River Settlement 1846-53,' in S. Marks and A. Atmore (eds.), *op. cit.*, 1980, 240.

CHAPTER 4

1. Extract from Richard Miller's letter of 1 June 1879, written from Morar in India, while serving with the 62nd Regiment Foot.

2. P. Spear, *India: a modern history*, Ann Arbor, 1972, 272.

3. O.H.K. Spate and A.T.A. Learmouth, *India and Pakistan: a general and regional geography*, London, 1972, 562.

4. *Ibid.*, 562-3.

5. *Ibid.*, 547.

6. John Doupe, a Palatine farmer from Courtmatrix, married the Millers' aunt, Rebecca Delmege of Killeheen on 15 April 1841. They had a family of four children before Rebecca's death in 1856, when she was aged thirty-nine.

7. D. Fitzpatrick, 'An ocean of consolation: letters and Irish immigration to Australasia,' in E. Richards et al. (eds.) *Visible immigrants: neglected sources for the history of Australian immigration*, Canberra, 1989, 60.

8. *Ibid.*, 60.

9. O.H.K. Spate and A.T.A. Learmouth, 1972, *op. cit.*, 52.

10. Richard Miller did in fact marry relatively soon afterwards. While still a serving soldier in Morar he passed the annual invaliding board for a change to England on 13 October 1880 and he married Miss A.E. Webb at Devizes in Wiltshire on 10 August 1881. Two daughters were born to them while Richard continued in army service, Janetta, 20/4/1884; and Rose, 25/7/1888. P.R.O., London, WO, 97/3468, 815.

11. As well as the Doupes of Courtmatrix, the Millers of Coolybrown also had close family connections with the Modlers and the Millers there.

12. Richard enjoyed a chequered army career. Having risen to the rank of color sergeant he was subsequently demoted to private in July 1884 when he was ' tried and sentenced to be reduced for making a fraudulent statement.' However, he later redeemed himself and was discharged in the rank of sergeant on 6 October 1889. Judging from his medical history, the last of his postings were in Ireland where he served in Longford (1887) and Athlone (1888-9). P.R.O., London, *op. cit.*

CHAPTER 5

1. Extract from a letter of Edward Miller's, written from the Australian bush on 26 September 1877, and addressed to his brother Robert at Coolybrown.

2. This much is apparent from the first of Christopher Miller's letters from South Africa.

3. P. O'Farrell, *The Irish in Australia*, Kensington, NSW, 1987, 85-6.

4. This is a reference to Thirza, the wife of James Winter and the sister of Barbara Miller.

5. P. O'Farrell, *Letters from Irish Australia*, Sydney, 1989.

6. See D. Fitzpatrick, ' That beloved country, that no place else resembles: connotations of Irishness in Irish- Australasian letters, 1841-1915,' *Irish Historical Studies* 27, no. 108, 1991, 347.

7. P. O'Farrell, 1987, *op. cit.*, 86.

8. J. Gentilli, ' Climate,' in D.N. Jeans (ed.), *Australia: a geography*, London, 1978, 7-37.

9. This is almost certainly Peter Miller of Ballycahane, Edward Miller's kinsman and brother of Anne Miller, who married into Coolybrown.

10. Sam Doupe, the son of John of Courtmatrix, was a first cousin of Edward Miller's. He was born on 5/7/1845.

11. P. O'Farrell, 1989, *op. cit.*, 19.

12. Ibid.; also D. Fitzpatrick, ' An ocean of consolation: letters and Irish immigration to Australasia,' in E. Richards et al. (eds.), *Visible immigrants: neglected sources for the history of Australian immigration*, Canberra, 1989, 83.

13. See page 39.

14. This reputedly Irish proverb is also cited by another emigrant, when writing home to his father in Co. Clare. See D. Fitzpatrick, 1989, *op. cit.*, 83.

15. All the indications suggest that this was the date on which Edward set off from Ireland on his long trip to Australia.

16. J.M. Powell, *The restive fringe: an historical geography of modern Australia*, Cambridge, 1988, 14.

17. P. O'Farrell, 1989, *op. cit.*, 46 et passim.

18. K.A. Miller, *Emigrants and exiles: Ireland and the Irish exodus to North America*, Oxford, 1985, 411.

19. K.W. Robinson, ' Space, politics and territorial organisation,' in D.N. Jeans (ed.), 1978, *op. cit.*, 368-9.

20. In an Australian context at this time, the job of tank making/ sinking may relate to the provision of increased water supplies. Initially water storage was improved by earth dams across creeks, then low-lying areas were excavated to provide storage for run-on waters as tanks. See R.L. Heathcote, ' Pastoral Australia,' in *ibid.*, 278.

21. For a detailed assessment of Ned Kelly, the man and the myth, see P. O'Farrell, 1987, *op. cit.*, 136-42.

22. R. Reece, 'Writing about the Irish in Australia,' in J. O'Brien and P. Travers (eds.), *The Irish emigrant experience in Australia*, Dublin, 1991, 229.

23. James Delmege was the son of Jacob and Eliza Delmege of Killeheen and a first cousin of Edward Miller's. He was born on 1 July 1852, and like Edward he set off for Australia.

24. For a useful summary, see W.J. Smyth, 'Social geography of rural Ireland: inventory and prospect,' in G.L. Davies (ed.), *Irish Geography Jubilee Volume*, Dublin, 1984, 210-2.

25. Like the Millers, the Neazors were a Palatine clan who had long struck roots in the townland of Ballycahane in Kilcornan parish. See P.J. O'Connor, *People make places: the story of the Irish Palatines*, Newcastle West, 1989, 147-8.

26. A. Marshall, ' Climate and primary production,' in D.N. Jeans (ed.), 1978, *op. cit.*, 237.

27. Sarah Gibbins also merits mention in James Hackett's letter to Robert Miller from New York city on 1 October 1884. See page 42.

28. John and Eliza Switzer of Courtmatrix had eight children born to them in the period 1858-75. Likeliest candidate for Queensland is John, baptised 21/1/1858, and if not him then Amos, born 5/10/1861.

29. Such horses would appear to have been in Ned's own keeping, as he indicated in an earlier letter to Peter Miller's mother (see page 90) that he dealt ' pretty heavy in horses.'

30. Mrs Magner was a relatively near neighbour of the Millers and it is apparent that prospective emigration was on her mind, presumably for a member of her family.

31. Jacob Delmege was the brother-in-law of James Winter.

32. Mary Anne Delmege emigrated to the United States *circa* 1883. See pp 40-1.

33. P. O'Farrell, 1989, *op. cit.*, 6.

34. For Canada, see J. Wreford Watson, ' Canadian regionalism in life and letters,' *The Geographical Journal* 131, 1, 1965, 28-9. For Australia see R.L. Heathcote, ' Pastoral Australia' in D.N. Jeans (ed.), 1978, *op. cit.*, 282.

35. Robert was the son of Jacob and Eliza Delmege of Killeheen. He was born on 23/3/1855.

36. This is a reference to Christopher, the first son of Robert and Anne Miller. He was born on 12/7/1882.

37. This was the same Sarah Miller who in 1883 was betrothed to Robert Delmege of Killeheen. However, she remained single until 3 March 1886 when she married instead Adam Miller of Garrenroe, Killonahan parish, near Croom.

38. For North America, see K.A. Miller, 1985. *op. cit.*; also D.H. Akenson, *Being had: historians, evidence, and the Irish in North America*, Port Credit, 1985, espec. 37-107. For Australia, see P. O'Farrell, 1987, *op. cit.*, espec. 54-114.

39. A. Marshall, in D.N. Jeans (ed.), 1978, *op. cit.*, 234-5.

40. R.L. Heathcote writes: ' From the shepherds and herders to the rouseabouts, boundary riders and jackeroos, and from the green ' new chums' to the experienced 'squatters' and 'graziers,' there was a spectrum of individual interest and expertise which varied not only between the jobs performed at any one time but over time itself. Most had no formal training before they took up their jobs, learning very much 'on the job' by watching how it was done by others, supposedly more experienced.' *Ibid.*, 271.

41. A brother of Sam's, he was born in April 1847.

42. Another of John Doupe's sons and a first cousin of the Millers of Coolybrown. He came to have an address at 190 Forbes St., Darlinghurst, Sydney.

43. It is likely that by this stage Ned's faithful companions were kelpies. Representing a cross between the smooth-haired Scotch collies with dingo-collie crosses, these were specially bred from the 1870s to withstand the difficult working conditions posed by hot summers, semi-wild livestock and the spiky grass awnlets and burrs of the plains. See R.L. Heathcote, in D.N. Jeans (ed.), 1978, *op. cit.*, 275.

44. Judging from later evidence, this would appear to be Louisa Delmege, another daughter of Jacob and Eliza of Killeheen. She was born on 25 April 1863.
45. For some twenty years from the early 1870s onwards, pastoral Australia came to be characterised by the widespread construction of boundary fences which were often - as was the case in Lachlan Downs Station - subsequently netted for rabbit proofing. See R.L. Heathcote, in D.N. Jeans (ed.), 1978, *op. cit.*, 275.
46. The Doupe farm in Courtmatrix in which Ned Miller had expressed an interest in July 1889 was sold eventually to John Thomas Preston. This Limerick city man had married Rebecca Delmege of Killeheen - yet another of Jacob's and Eliza's daughters in 1881 - and thus there were kin linkages with the Doupes of Courtmatrix and the Millers of Coolybrown.
47. Whatever about Ned Miller's earlier glowing optimism concerning Albany and Western Australia, both Albany and Bunbury were described as 'miserable holes' by an Irish immigrant in 1891. See P. O'Farrell, 1989, *op. cit.*, 83.

CHAPTER 6
1. A throwaway note, barely decipherable and written on the back of a notebook *circa* 1900.
2. Sentiments expressed by Christopher Miller in a letter of 15 September 1947, written to his sister Rose from the Liverpool area of New South Wales. Christy died in Australia the following year.
3. Miller family returns, ' Form A,' *Census of Ireland 1901*, Coolybrown townland, Kilscannell parish, Lower Connello barony.
4. See page 96.
5. Mary Daly and Willie Ruttle married in 1938, Willie having turned Catholic in order to marry.
6. The Limerick & Tralee branch of the railway cut transversely across the southern portion of Coolybrown in close proximity to the Miller farm.
7. M. Turner, ' Rural economies in post-Famine Ireland, *c.* 1850-1914,' in B.J. Graham and L.J. Proudfoot (eds.), *An historical geography of Ireland*, London, 1993, 327-30.
8. Originally from Courtmatrix, Lizzie Preston was the daughter of John Thomas Preston and Rebecca Delmege and thus was related to the Millers of Coolybrown through the Delmege line. Like her aunt, Mary Anne Delmege, she emigrated to the Lowell area of Massachusetts where she married, had a young family, and was then tragically widowed. She subsequently became a nurse and showed considerable resourcefulness by raising her family on her own.
9. See page 96.
10. See page 108.
11. The Odells feature in the correspondence of Edward Miller. See page 103.
12. Whether through increased rent demand or outright eviction is not known.
13. The first World War was ended by armistice on 11 November 1918.
14. Like the Millers and Listons of Coolybrown, the Corbetts of Skehanagh were long-time residents in the area, with a record of occupancy going back to at least the first half of the nineteenth century.
15. This much is clear from a letter of Christy Miller's in September 1947. He had an address at 1934 E. 47th Street, Brooklyn, New York.

16. P. Scott, ' Rural land use,' in D.N. Jeans (ed.), *Australia: a geography*, London, 1978, 212-3.
17. After the old father's death, Ned, the elder of the two brothers at home, would have taken over as 'the new boss.'
18. Jack's one-eight share went to the master of the hospital, while Emily's was divided equally between her sons Robert and William.

Epilogue
1. P.J. O'Connor, *People make places; the story of the Irish Palatines*, Newcastle West, 1989, 196.
2. In relation to wake practices among the Palatines, it is worth noting the observations of P.W. Joyce a century earlier. See, *ibid.*, 125.
3. Reen's Pike, where the Ardagh and Newcastle West roads diverge on the way from Rathkeale, is usually abbreviated as the ' Pike ' in local parlance. The term derives from the turnpike roads of eighteenth century Ireland. See J.H. Andrews, ' Road planning in Ireland before the railway age,' *Irish Geography* 5, 1, 1964, 23-6.
4. Ned's camp bed fitted snugly into the wall in an alcove in the upper room.
5. Some time after Rosie died, Ned Ruttle, a nephew of the Miller brothers, came to live with them and care for them. He later inherited the place.

Index